I0494528

NOVEMBER 20, 2015

Dear Teachers,

This guide was written and designed to highlight exceptional works in the BMA's collection of African art, now on view in the recently renovated African art galleries. Objects are grouped into suites to allow teachers and students to explore aesthetic and thematic connections, as well as diversity of artistic expression. Each lesson is accompanied by classroom activities that support standards of learning and prompt exciting student investigations into key aspects of the artworks.

There are a total of five lessons in this resource and they each contain the following:
- Full-color images of artworks
- Key Topics: A list of key topics to highlight important concepts in the text
- Close Looking: An exploration of the artworks' visual elements
- Art in Context: Information on the multiple contexts (historical, art historical, social, economic, geographic, etc.) in which the art was produced
- Classroom Activities: Experiences that lead students in close looking and engage them with the important ideas and techniques introduced through the featured artworks
- Standards and Curriculum: A list of relevant standards from the Common Core State Standards and Maryland State Curriculum

All lessons support the following 21st-Century Skills:
- Communication and Collaboration
- Creativity and Innovation
- Critical Thinking and Problem Solving
- Flexibility and Adaptability
- Initiative and Self-Direction
- Leadership and Responsibility
- Productivity and Accountability
- Social and Cross-Cultural Skills

Please note that works of art at the BMA rotate. If you plan to bring students to the Museum, be sure to call ahead to confirm that particular artworks are on view. We hope you and your students enjoy this guide as you explore remarkable works from the BMA's collection of African art.

SUZY WOLFFE & ELIZABETH BENSKIN

ACKNOWLEDGMENTS

PROJECT DIRECTOR AND CLASSROOM ACTIVITIES WRITER
Elizabeth Benskin,
Director of School and Teacher Programs

RESEARCHER AND WRITER
Suzy Wolffe,
Manager of School Programs

Design by G. Brockett Horne and Micah Wood

Special thanks to Kathryn Wysocki Gunsch, former BMA curator of African art; Anne Manning, former Deputy Director for Education and Interpretation; Michelle Boardman, Director of Integrated Media Initiatives; and Aden Weisel, former Curatorial Assistant, Arts of Africa, the Americas, Asia & the Pacific Islands; for their input and support. The BMA would also like to thank the following local teachers and teachers-in-training, who offered extremely helpful feedback on the project:

Jaye Ayres	Visual Arts Resource Teacher, Howard County Public Schools
Gino Molfino	Fine Arts Coordinator, Howard County Public Schools
Katie Atkinson	Art Teacher, Thunder Hill Elementary School
Alexandra Borleis	Art Teacher, Long Reach High School
Sonya Everett	Art Teacher, Marriotts Ridge High School
Danielle Klim	Art Teacher, Reservoir High School
Christine Long	Art Teacher, Reservoir High School
Rachel Ludlow	Art Teacher, Thomas Viaduct Middle School
Brendan Mruk	Art Teacher, Wilde Lake High School
Pari Papaioannu	Art Teacher, Bellows Spring Elementary School & Phelps Luck Elementary School
Sarah Ross	Art Teacher, Northfield and Hammond Elementary School
Michele Schroder	Art Teacher, Manor Woods Elementary School & Rockburn Elementary School
Blair Spangenthal	Art Teacher, Worthington Elementary School & Laurel Woods Elementary School
Ben Shipley	Art Teacher, Hammond Middle School
Shannon Townsend	Art Teacher, Elkridge Landing Middle School
Lang Wethington	Art Teacher, Wilde Lake Middle School

The Baltimore Museum of Art Teacher's Guide to the African Collection has been made possible in part by a major grant from the National Endowment for the Humanities: Celebrating 50 Years of Excellence. This project is supported in part by an award from the National Endowment for the Arts.

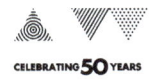 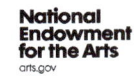 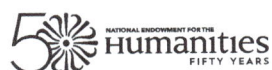

TABLE OF CONTENTS

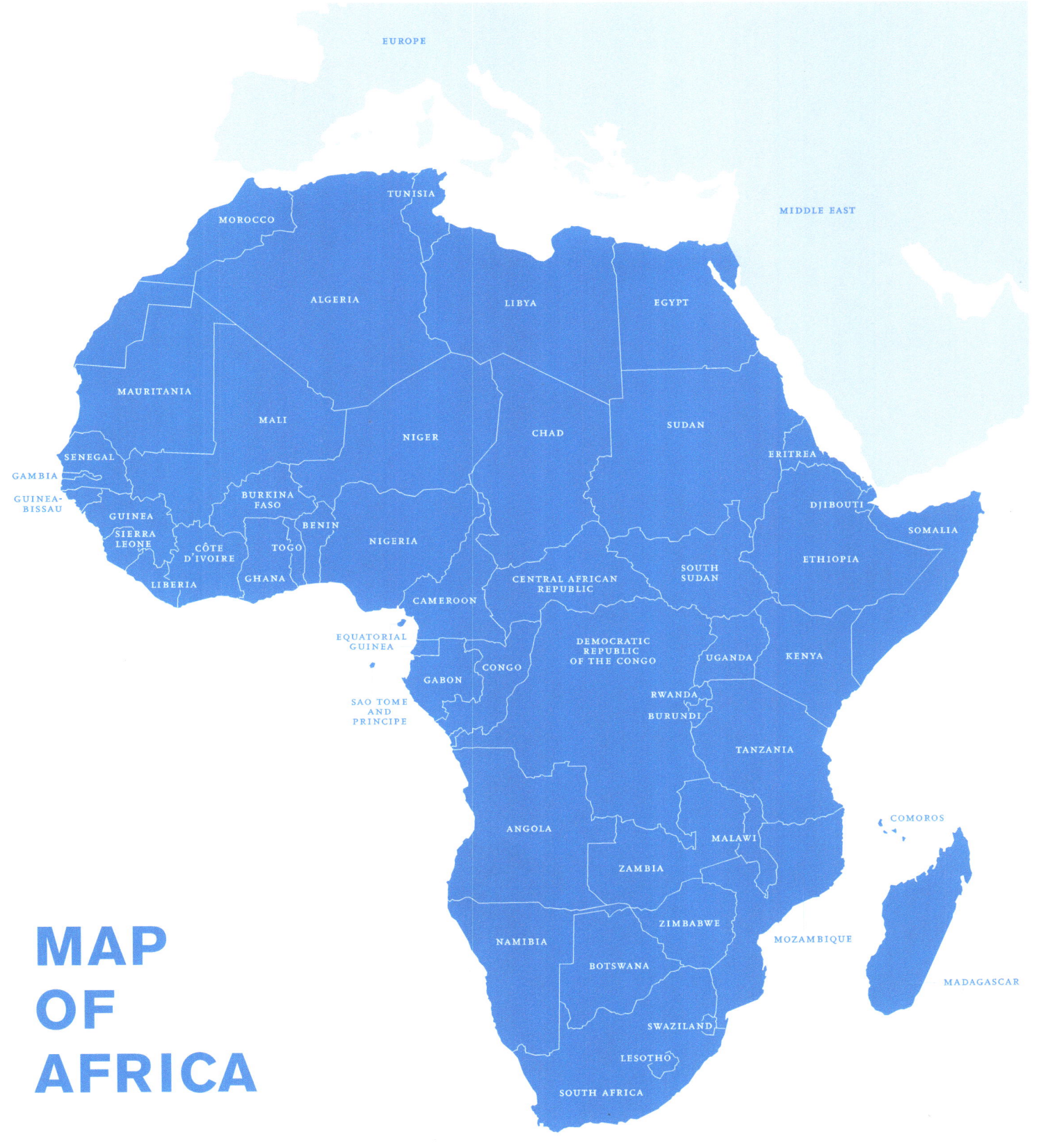

MAP
OF
AFRICA

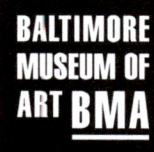

FACES OF ORDER AND CHAOS

KEY TERMS
- Conflict Resolution
- Headdress
- Mask
- Public Masquerade
- Role Models

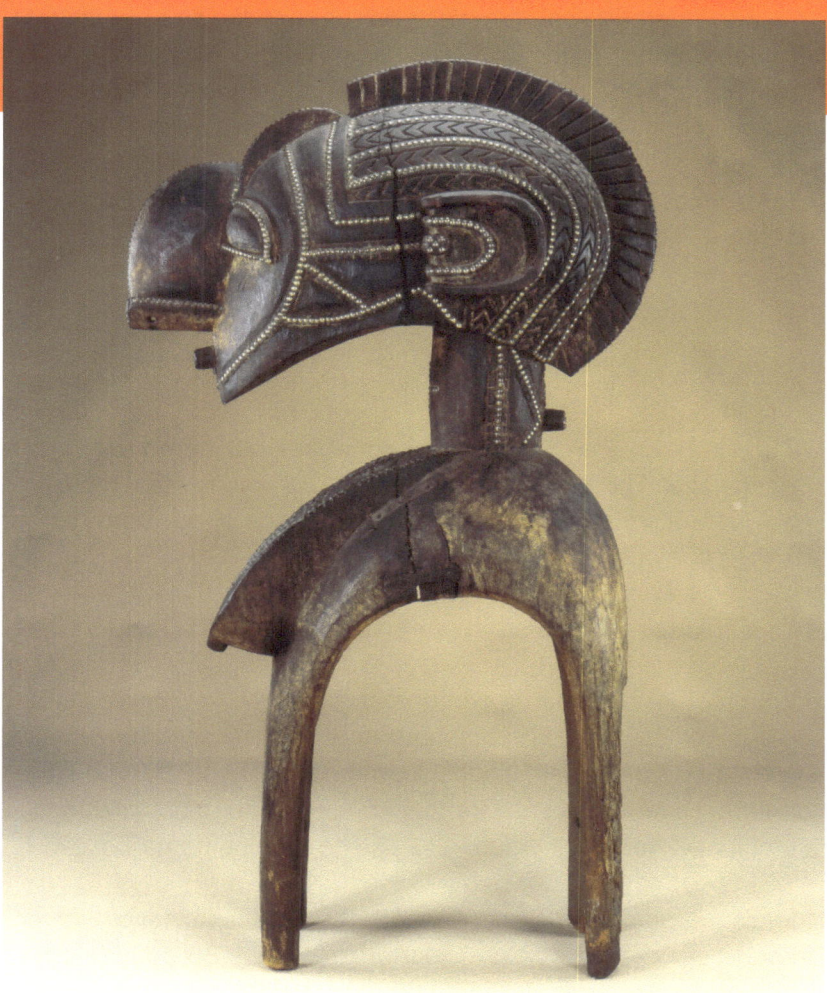

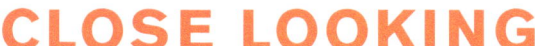

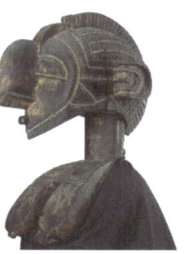

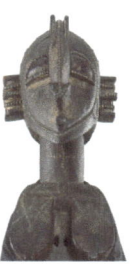

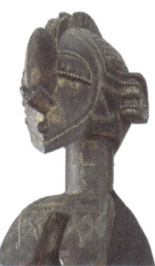

GREAT MOTHER HEADDRESS (D'MBA) Late 19th-early 20th century

Artist Unidentified
Baga region, possibly Monchon village, Guinea
Wood, copper alloy tacks, and iron tacks
Gift of Alan Wurtzburger, BMA 1957.97

CLOSE LOOKING

FOR THE BAGA PEOPLE on the northern coast of Guinea and the southern coast of Guinea-Bissau, D'mba, or Great Mother, represents ideal female beauty both physically and in her role as a dutiful mother. D'mba (pronounced DIMbah) wears an elegant hairstyle with braids carved in precise parallel rows. Seen in profile, a crest along the center of her semi-circular head creates a series of curvilinear lines that proceed down over her forehead and rise again to the end of her nose.

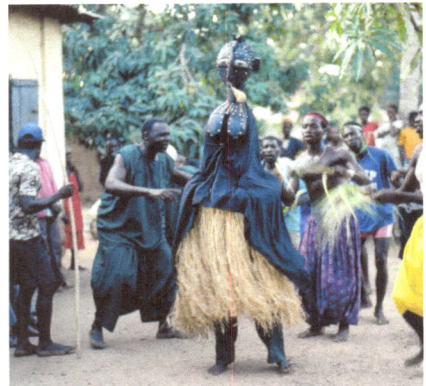

**Baga region,
possibly Monchon village,
Guinea**

Dancing D'mba Baga Sitem, Guinea.
Photo: Frederick John Lamp, 1990

D'MBA IN PERFORMANCE

Africanist scholar and curator Frederick Lamp described a performance as follows:

"The dance of the D'mba begins with the appearance of a line of drummers dancing while beating their drums, in single file, followed by the D'mba dancer…. D'mba executes both sedate and vigorous steps, sometimes twirling, now pacing delicately, occasionally lying down completely on the ground, helped by assistants, and then standing up again. The crowd cheers wildly after D'mba floats around the perimeter of the circle, suddenly whirls around, and stops suddenly."[2]

Her physical features include large eyes, C-shaped ears, an arrow-shaped nose (when seen frontally), long and slender neck, large flat breasts, and a small protruding mouth. Her wooden surface gleams with high polish, and brass tacks highlight her facial features and braids. Tacks create patterns on her neck and breasts that imitate decorative scarring. These patterns include single and parallel lines, V shapes, and crosses. Between her breasts are small holes that allowed dancers of the D'mba to see through the mask. Standing on four supports that would have rested on the dancer's shoulders, and carved from a single piece of wood, the massive headdress stands just over four feet high and weighs over 80 pounds. Resting on the head of the dancer, D'mba would appear as an immensely tall and stately figure.

ART IN CONTEXT

PUBLIC MASQUERADES IN SOME AFRICAN SOCIETIES communicate valued behaviors and discourage activities considered unhealthy or antisocial. The three headdresses in this lesson are used in masquerades to communicate the importance of duty and harmony or to warn against the danger of chaos.

Not a spiritual entity, but rather a role model, D'mba represents the ideal woman in Baga (pronounced BAHgah) society. Selflessly, the Great Mother has embraced her maternal duty. Prominent flattened breasts indicate that she bore and nursed many children, whom she has guided to become productive members of society. The large scale of her eyes and ears indicate that she sees and hears all things in her community; her small mouth tells us she refrains from gossiping.

In masquerade, D'mba was danced by young men, never women, in part because the colossal headdress weighs 83 pounds. She appeared only during daylight hours, when she presided over weddings, planting and harvesting ceremonies, and funerals. Before every performance, she was polished and her tacks were shined to flash in the sun. D'mba would have been clothed in a costume of palm fibers, called raffia, and a dark cloth cape that hid the mask's supporting posts. Dancers rested her heavy weight on a cloth pad covering their heads and gripped the mask by its front posts. During the masquerade, D'mba was surrounded by a circle of men from her clan group with women forming an outer circle. Her imposing figure, engaged in a dramatic and elegant dance, was intended to set a moral and behavioral standard for all men and women in the community. For the Baga, D'mba's dance was a favorite among masquerades.[1] Her performance was accompanied by musicians playing two kinds of drums, a slit gong, and sometimes antelope horn trumpets.

Baga culture began to erode when France colonized the land in the 1890s, and Roman Catholics began to convert the Baga. The loss of tradition was aggravated in 1958 when Guinea won its independence from France, under the newly formed Muslim government. The new regime confiscated and destroyed Baga cultural artifacts and forbade non-Muslim religious practices. This political situation continued until 1984, when Guinea's first president, who ruled since 1958, died. Elements of Baga culture slowly began to reemerge. In the 1980s, some Baga performances were revitalized under the direction of Baga villagers who had participated in the events prior to 1958.

RELATED ARTWORK

FOR THE WÈ (PRONOUNCED WAY) PEOPLE, the Gbona Gla (pronounced gBOHnah glah), or Mask of Wisdom, appears infrequently, but when it does, it performs the crucial roles of maintaining community harmony and warning of chaos lurking outside the village. The heavily wooded area in which the Wè reside extends from southwest Côte d'Ivoire to eastern Liberia, and the community makes a clear distinction between the safety of the village and the danger of the surrounding forest, inhabited by wild animals and malevolent spirits.[3] Gbona Gla, with his bright red face and bulging eyes, represents the forest's uncontrollable forces.

The maker of the mask included physical characteristics of various animals to harness their combined spiritual power. Included in the mask are bird feathers, wild bush cat fur wrapped around a yellow spike under the nose, long animal hair, blue warthog horns, and carved spikes resembling sharp leopard teeth that form a ruff around the mask. Decorated with commercial paint, the mask draws the viewer's eye to the intense primary colors of red, blue, and yellow. The white paint acts as a strong contrast that causes the already tubular eyes and bulging forehead to pop out. Together these features exaggerate the fierce strength of the spirit.

The Mask of Wisdom emerges when a community leader must intervene in a serious conflict because all other means to remedy the situation have been exhausted. Reflecting the gravity of the threat to community stability when conflicts remain unresolved, the verdict of the Gbona Gla is always final.[4] The Mask of Wisdom acts as a reminder that peace in the community creates order, and that the order of civilization prevents evil spirits of the forest from encroaching upon the village.

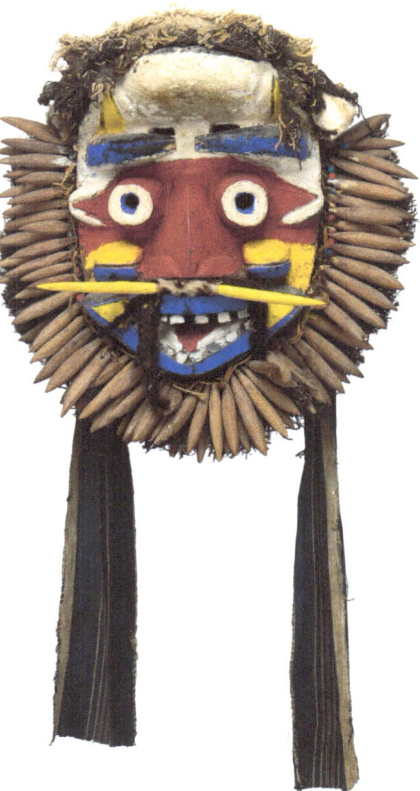

MASK OF WISDOM (GBONA GLA)
Mid-20th century

Artist unidentified
Wè region, Côte d'Ivoire or Liberia
Wood, paint, cloth, fur, glass beads, hair, plant fibers, and iron
Gift of Dr. and Mrs. Bernard Berk and Mr. and Mrs. Leonard Whitehouse, BMA 1969.11

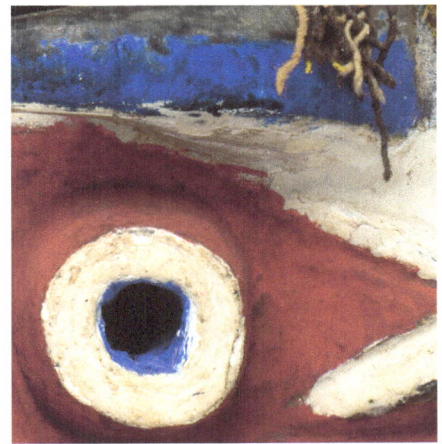

Detail of Mask of Wisdom

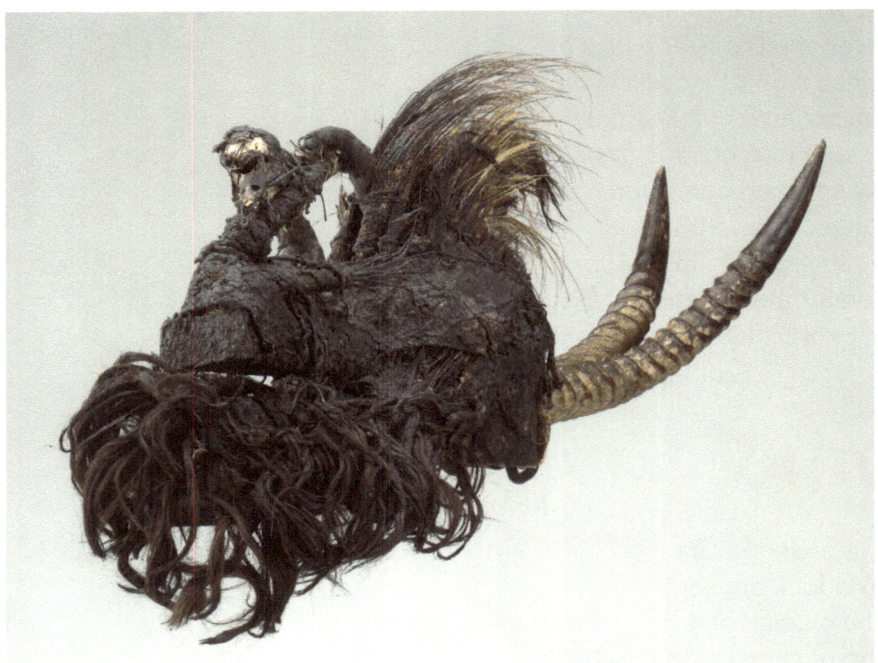

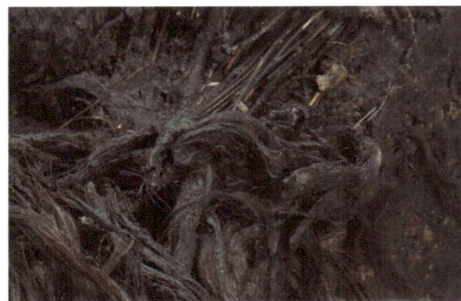

Detail of Kòmò Society Helmet Mask

KÒMÒKUN (pronounced kohMOHkin) is an object of terror. This Kòmò (pronounced KOHmoh) headdress, belonging to the Manding peoples of Mali and Guinea, performs two critical roles: divining answers that will resolve community issues and frightening the young male initiates of the secret Kòmò Society—the most respected and feared of all male associations in the area—into proper behavior.[5] The mask is made by a Kòmò Society blacksmith who, because he forges iron with fire, is said to be able to harness dangerous power for communal good.

The wooden headdress is carved and then embellished with various objects to capture their individual power. A wide and open jaw that bears sharp teeth is thought to symbolize a hyena, an animal whose jaw is strong enough to eat most living things. It represents Kòmò Society's power to "devour" rule breakers. The animal is also thought to have vast knowledge of the wilderness and thus to be able to impart wisdom to the wearer.[6] Large curved horns extend from the back of the mask, and porcupine quills—signifying aggression—protrude from the top. In addition, fiber, glass, earth rendered spiritually powerful by the blacksmith, and layer upon layer of sacrificial animal blood and millet increase its power. The bird skull on the mask is significant because birds are masters of both land and air. The skull harnesses both energies that are then channeled through the wearer.[7]

Kòmòkun is masqueraded at night under the light of the moon or by bonfire. Low light levels and the mask's assemblage of parts make it difficult to see clearly, amplifying the fear that surrounds it. The costume worn by the masker consists of a loose cotton gown to which feathers of a vulture—credited with bringing Kòmò knowledge to earth—are attached.[8] The masquerade is preceded by a shrill whistle that warns women, young children, and uninitiated males to lock themselves in their houses and not peer upon Kòmòkun for fear of death.[9] The masker is guided because he is unable to see out of the mask, and he is accompanied by ominous drumming and a cacophony of gongs, whistles, drums, cymbals, and horns.[10] The masker himself is possessed by a spirit and, in a distorted voice, Kòmòkun provides answers to the issues presented to it.[11] The masker is accompanied by an interpreter, called the "Mouth of the Beast," who translates his wisdom.

Following circumcision, Kòmò initiates see Kòmòkun for the first time. The event is designed to terrify these new society members into behaving properly and to prepare them to be brave in the everyday world. Initiates must peer into the jaws of the dreadful mask, after which they are forced to lick Kòmòkun three times and swear they will put the Kòmò above all else in their lives, thus ensuring compliance to community rules.[12]

THE DAN (pronounced dahn) people of Liberia awarded a man who excelled at clearing fields for farmers with his team of workers. Because he worked faster and harder than others, he was honored with the Champion Brush Cutter's Hat, made of various plant fibers and feathers. The hat is an emblem of respect for his outstanding contribution to the community. For more information on the Brush Cutter's Hat see http://www.artbma.org/documents/atg/pdf/ATG_10-11.pdf in the Art-to-Go resource section of the BMA website.

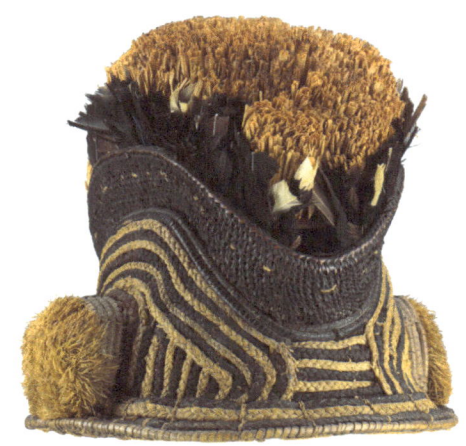

CHAMPION BRUSH CUTTER'S HAT
Early 20th century

Artist Unidentified
Dan region, Côte d'Ivoire or Liberia
Plant fibers and feathers
Gift of Catherine O'Carroll Bussell and Robert Bruce Bussell, Arlington, Virginia, BMA 1998.437

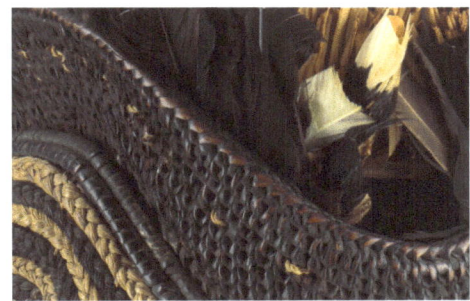

Detail of Champion Brush Cutter's Hat

[1] Frederick John Lamp, *Art of the Baga: A Drama of Cultural Reinvention* (New York: The Museum for African Art, 1996), 156.

[2] Frederick John Lamp, "Sun, Fire, and Variations on Womanhood: a Baga/Bulunits Mask (D'mba)," in *See the Music Hear the Dance*, ed. Frederick John Lamp (Munich: Prestel Publishing, 2004), 222.

[3] "Wè," University of Iowa Museum of Art, accessed January 12, 2015, http://africa.uima.uiowa.edu/peoples/show/We.

[4] Marie-Noël Verger-Fèvre, "Mask of Wisdom: a Wè Mask (Gbona Gla)," in *See the Music Hear the Dance*, ed. Frederick John Lamp (Munich: Prestel Publishing, 2004), 42.

[5] Sarah Brett-Smith, "The Mouth of the Komo," *RES: Anthropology and Aesthetics* 31 (Spring 1997), 72.

[6] Ibid., 80.

[7] "Bamana Komo (Komokun) Helmut Masks," accessed January 12, 2015, http://www.randafricanart.com/Bamana_Komo_headdress.html.

[8] Frederick John Lamp, "You Haven't Seen the Wild Beast: a Manding Headdress (Komo Kun)," in *See the Music Hear the Dance*, ed. Frederick John Lamp (Munich: Prestel Publishing, 2004), 235.

[9] Brett-Smith, "The Mouth of the Komo," 77.

[10] Lamp, "You Haven't Seen the Beast," 234.

[11] Brett-Smith, 76.

[12] Ibid., 89.

CLASSROOM ACTIVITIES

ACTIVITY 1:
Exploring Roles and Responsibilities
Grades: K–2, 3–5
Subjects: English Language Arts, History/Social Studies, Visual Arts

The teacher will display images of the Great Mother Headdress (D'mba), the Mask of Wisdom (Gbona Gla), and the Champion Brush Cutter's Hat and ask students a series of questions about each object:

- What colors do you see?
- What shapes do you see?
- What textures do you see?
- What forms do you see?
- What materials do you think these artworks might be made from?

The teacher will share information about each object, focusing on the way the artworks were intended to celebrate being a good member of the community (Great Mother Headdress [D'mba], Champion Brush Cutter's Hat) or to resolve concerns and conflicts to ensure the community's wellbeing (Mask of Wisdom [Gbon Gla]).

The teacher will then divide students into pairs and ask them to discuss the following question:

- What is one thing you can do to be a good member of 1) the class, 2) the school, and 3) the community?

After students have discussed their ideas, they will share with the class. The teacher will record student responses on the black/white board. The teacher may add ideas of his/her own and moderate if there are disagreements about whether certain ideas support being a good member of the community.

Providing colored pencils and/or markers and paper, and leaving previous responses visible, the teacher will ask students to draw pictures of themselves contributing to the class in one positive way. Each student's drawing may be placed near his/her desk or around the room as a daily reminder to the class. The activity can be repeated and pictures added over time.

ACTIVITY 2:
Connecting Visual Art and Classroom Culture
Grades: 3–5
Subjects: English Language Arts, History/ Social Studies, Visual Arts

The teacher will divide students into groups of four. Each group will be asked to look at one of the following images: Great Mother Headdress (D'mba), the Mask of Wisdom (Gbon Gla), the Kòmò Society Helmet Mask (Kòmòkun), and the Champion Brush Cutter's Hat. The teacher will ask students to write down as many things as they can observe about their group's artwork in three minutes. When the time is up, groups will have several minutes to share their observations and make a master list. As a class, students will be asked to share their observations, focusing on the art elements:

- What colors do you see?
- What shapes do you see?
- What textures do you see?
- What forms do you see?
- What materials do you think these artworks might be made from?

As each group presents its observations, the teacher will give information about the meaning and context of the artwork.

Each group will be asked to select a recorder and collaboratively make a list of what a healthy class culture looks like (i.e. respectful, caring, honest, etc). They will share their ideas with the class, while the teacher records the responses on a black/white board. Each student will receive four small post-it notes and and place the post-it notes next to the four ideas that they think are most important for a healthy class community. The teacher will tally the four ideas with the most post-it notes.

Student groups will be randomly assigned to one of the four top descriptors for a healthy class culture. Using large sheets of white or butcher paper and pencils, colored pencils, markers, and/or collage materials and glue sticks, each group will design and create a poster to promote the idea. The teacher will guide students by asking them to discuss and agree upon their understanding of the idea, talk about the best way to visually express the idea, sketch the design, and, finally, make the poster.

When posters are complete, student groups will share their work with the class, explaining the artistic choices they made to convey the theme. The teacher can ask students to observe and remark upon similarities and differences in the visual expressions of the ideas. Posters can then be displayed in the classroom.

STANDARDS AND CURRICULUM

COMMON CORE STATE STANDARDS

English Language Arts
Grade 1
CCSS.ELA-Literacy.SL.1.1. Participate in collaborative conversations with diverse partners about grade 1 topics and texts with peers and adults in small and larger groups.

Grade 2
CCSS.ELA-Literacy.SL.2.1. Participate in collaborative conversations with diverse partners about grade 2 topics and texts with peers and adults in small and larger groups.

Grade 3
CCSS.ELA-Literacy.SL.3.1. Engage effectively in a range of collaborative discussions (one-on-one, in groups, and teacher-led) with diverse partners on grade 3 topics and texts, building on others' ideas and expressing their own clearly.

MARYLAND STATE CURRICULUM

History/Social Studies
Grade 1
1.C.1.a. Identify the rights, responsibilities, and choices that students have in the family, school, and neighborhood.
2.C.1.a. Describe, discuss, and demonstrate appropriate social skills necessary for working in a cooperative group, such as sharing concern, care, and respect among group members.

Grade 2
1.A.1.a. Explain how school and community rules promote orderliness, fairness, responsibility, privacy, and safety.
1.C.1.a. Recognize and describe how making choices affects self, family, school, and community.
2.C.1.a. Identify and demonstrate appropriate social skills necessary for working in a cooperative group, such as sharing concern, care, and respect among group members.
2.C.1.b. Analyze how different points of view in school situations may result in compromise or conflict.

Grade 3
1.C.1.a. Describe the responsibilities of being an effective citizen, such as cleaning up your neighborhood, being informed, obeying rules and laws, participating in class discussions, and volunteering.
2.C.1.a. Identify and demonstrate appropriate social skills necessary for working in a cooperative group, such as sharing concern, compassion, and respect among group members.
2.C.1.b. Analyze how different points of view in school and community situations may result in compromise or conflict.

Visual Arts
Grade 1
1.2.b. Use color, line, shape, texture, and form to represent ideas visually from observation, memory, and imagination.
1.3.a. Explore and discuss the qualities of color, line, shape, texture, and form in artworks.
2.1.a. Observe works of art and identify ways that artists express ideas about people, places, and events.

Grade 2
1.1.a. Describe colors, lines, shapes, textures, forms, and space found in observed objects and the environment.
1.2.a. Describe how artists use color, line, shape, texture, form, and space to represent ideas visually from observation, memory, and imagination.
2.1.a. Observe works of art and describe how artists express ideas about people, places, and events.
2.2.b. Communicate a variety of reasons for creating artworks, such as feelings, experiences, events, places, and ideas.

Grade 3
1.1.a. Describe similarities and differences between the elements of art in observed forms.
1.2.a. Compare and describe how artists communicate what they see, know, feel, and imagine using art vocabulary.
1.2.b. Represent ideas and feelings visually that describe what is seen, felt, known, and imagined.
1.3.a. Describe how the elements of art and principles of design are organized to communicate personal meaning in visual compositions.
2.3.a. Discuss and compare how selected artworks from different times or cultures are similar or different (e.g. common themes, content, form, and style).

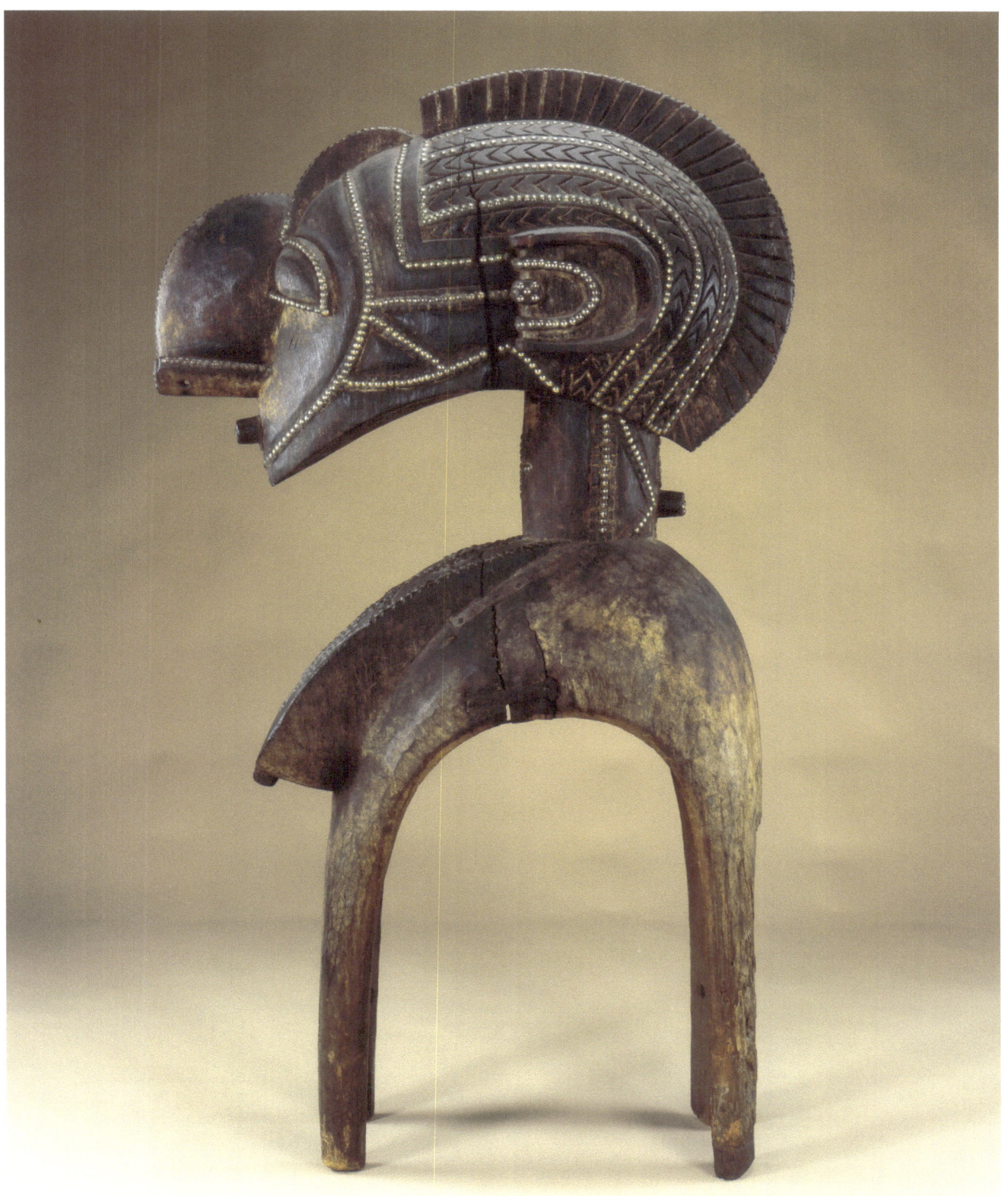

Great Mother Headdress (D'mba). Late 19th–early 20th century. Baga region, possibly Monchon village, Guinea. Wood, copper alloy tacks, and iron tacks. Gift of Alan Wurtzburger, BMA 1957.97

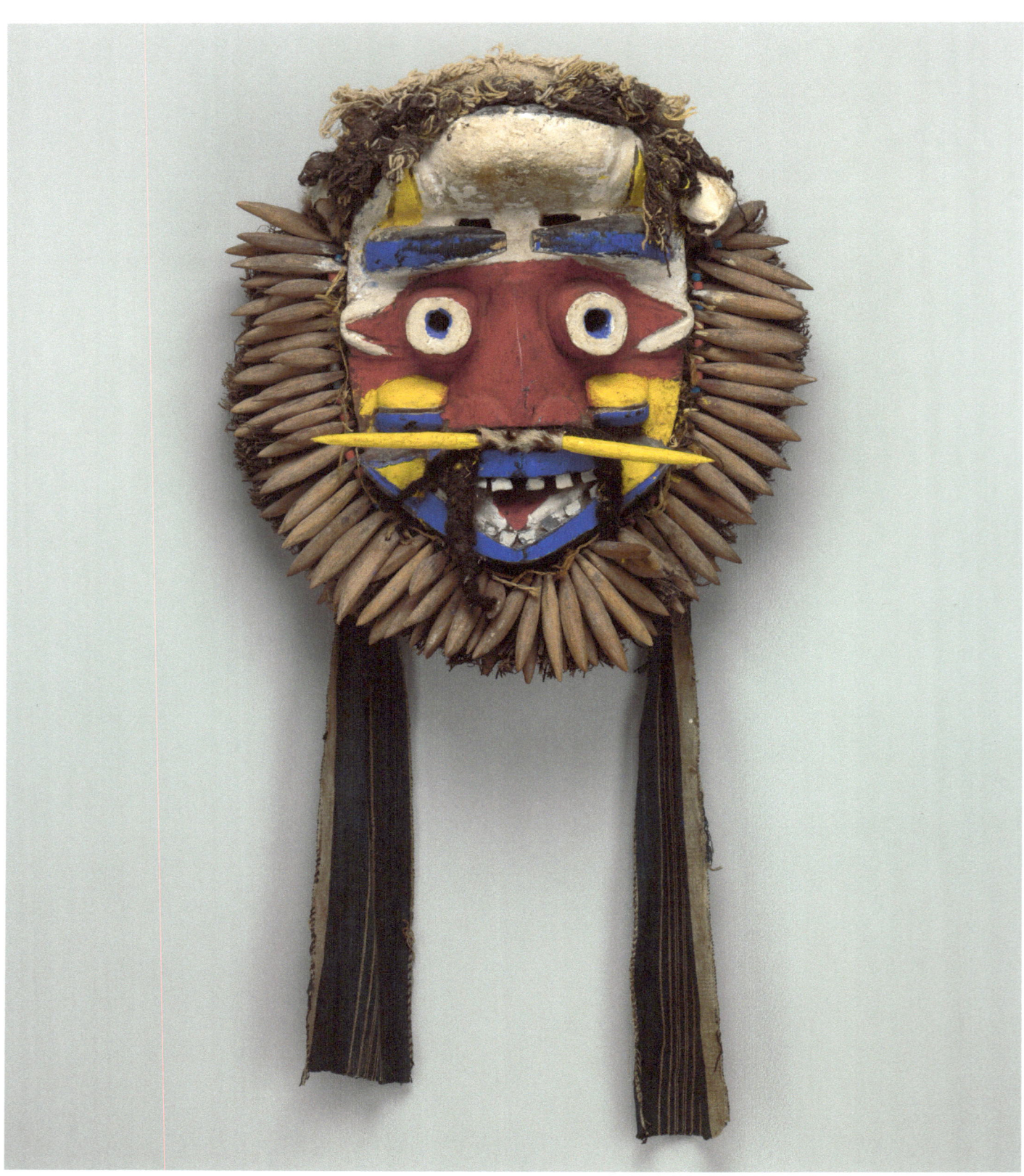

Mask of Wisdom (Gbona Gla). Mid-20th century. Wè region, Côte d'Ivoire or Liberia. Wood, paint, cloth, fur, glass beads, hair, plant fibers, and iron teeth. Gift of Dr. and Mrs. Bernard Berk and Mr. and Mrs. Leonard Whitehouse, BMA 1969.11

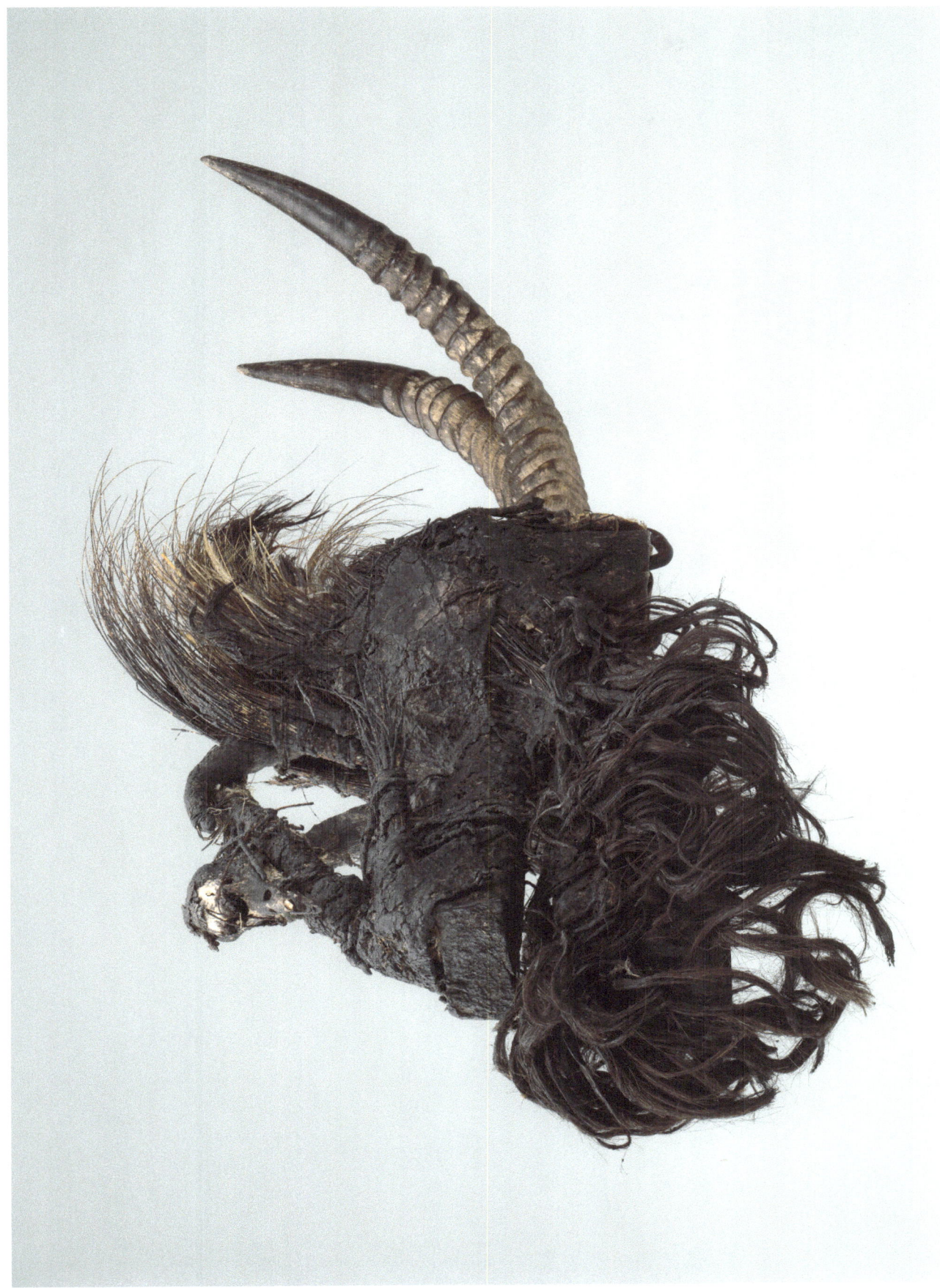

Kòmò Society Helmet Mask (Kòmòkun). Early 20th century. Manding or Minianka region, Mali or Guinea. Wood, animal horns, bird skull, plant fibers, porcupine quills, earth, and glass. Gift of Robert and Mary Cumming, Baltimore, BMA 1983.79

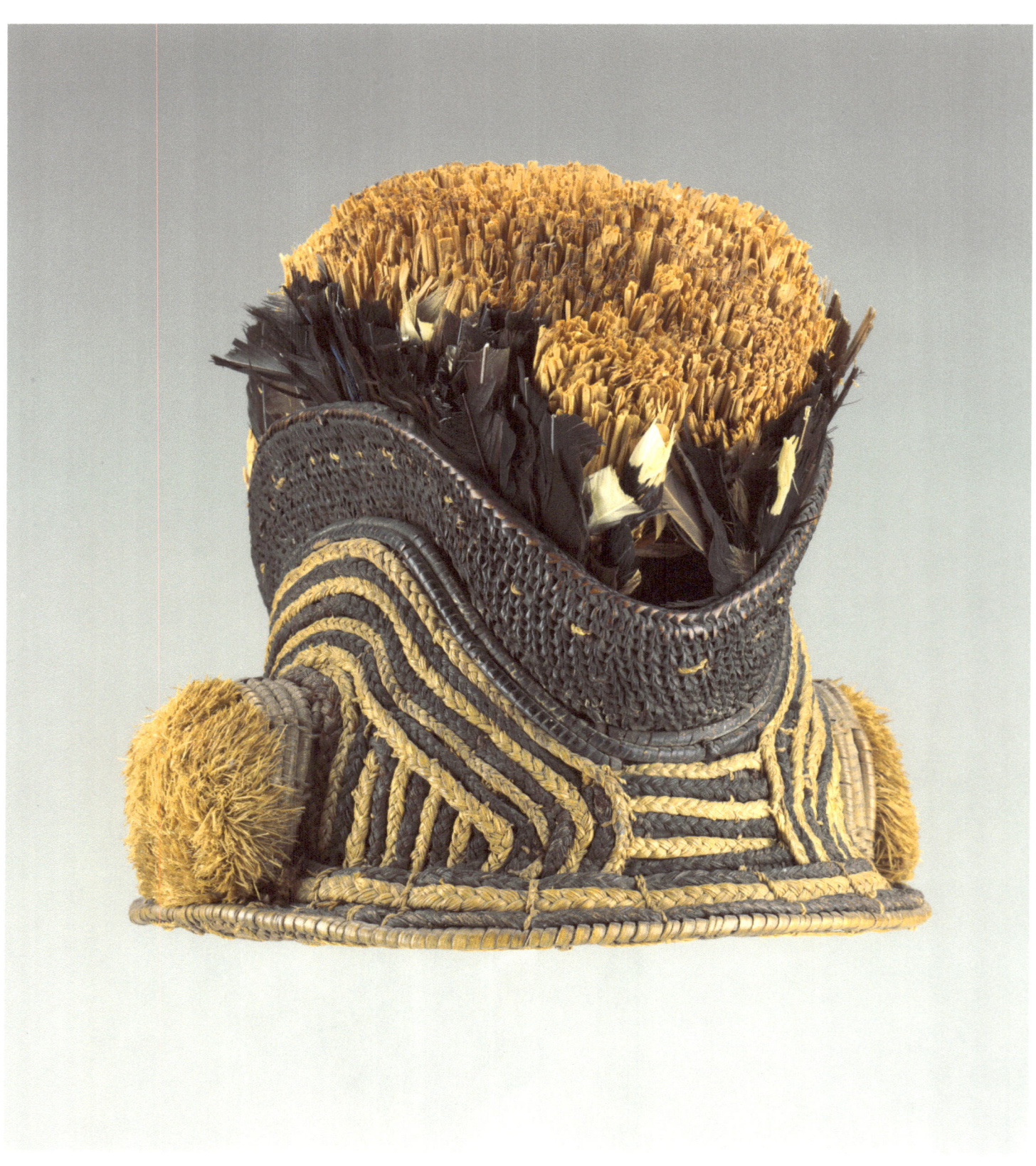

Champion Brush Cutter's Hat. Early 20th century. Dan region, Côte d'Ivoire or Liberia. Plant fibers and feathers. Gift of Catherine O'Carroll Bussell and Robert Bruce Bussell, Arlington, Virginia, BMA 1998.437

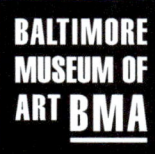
STYLE AND MEANING

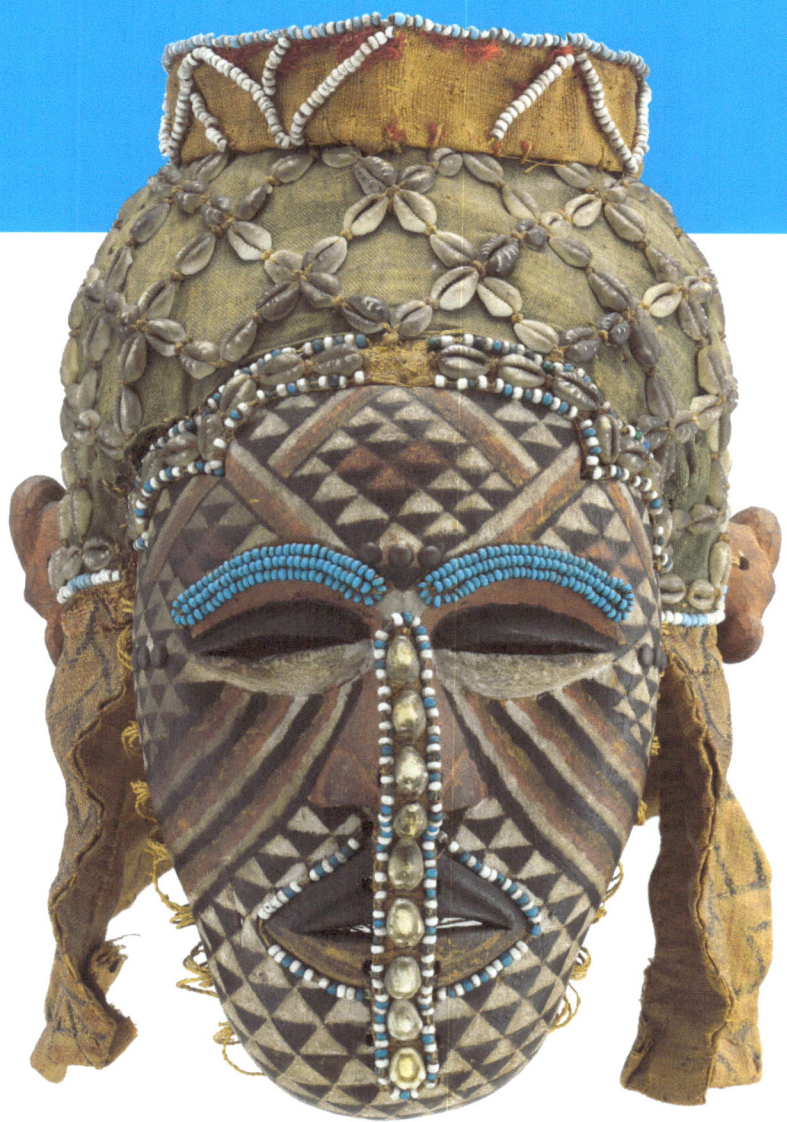

CLOSE LOOKING

MANY OF THE SYMMETRICAL BEADED, painted, and woven motifs covering the face and neck of Ngaady Mwaash (pronounced enGAdee mwash), meaning "the woman of Mwaash," are borrowed from the linear and geometric patterns of textiles made by the Kuba people of the Democratic Republic of the Congo.[1] One complicated design of alternating black and white painted triangles is called "the

FEMALE MASK (NGAADY MWAASH)

Late 19th–early 20th century

Artist Unidentified
Kuba kingdom, Democratic Republic of the Congo
Wood, cloth, copper alloy tacks, plant fibers, cowrie shells, glass beads, and paint
Gift of Alan Wurtzburger, BMA 1954.145.77

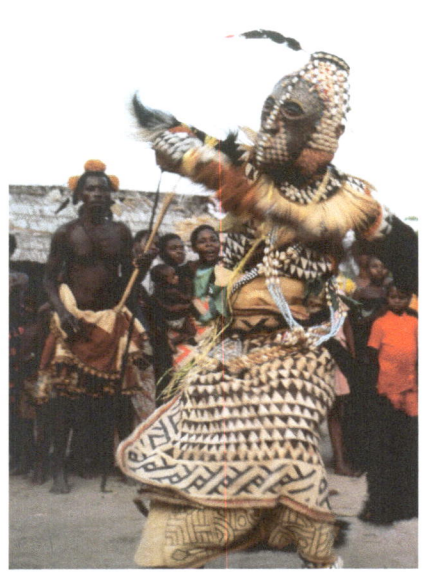

Ngady Mwaash performs at a funeral.
Southern Kuba, community of Boganciala,
Congo (Kinshasa).
Photo: Patricia Darish and David A. Binkley, 1982

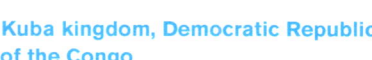

**Kuba kingdom, Democratic Republic
of the Congo**

king's house," a reference to the royal status of Mweel (pronounced mWHEEL), first queen of the Kuba kingdom, whom Ngaady Mwaash embodies. Other designs include a lattice-patterned hairstyle made of cowrie shells, a material used in African trade that symbolizes status and wealth. As is the case with many royal masks, the nose and mouth of Ngaady Mwaash are hidden behind a band of cloth decorated with alternating blue and white beads that flank a row of cowrie shells. This band falls from the bridge of the nose down and over the chin. Three parallel lines of turquoise beads form the eyebrows. Red, white, and black stripes running from the mask's eyes to the jawline are called "tears" and may reference tears shed at funerals.

The mask's carved wood face is attached to a cloth-covered framework—including two wooden ears—that forms the top, back, and sides of the head. A triangular hat recalls those worn by female diviners of the Kuba people. Its inclusion suggests the relationship between Ngaady Mwaash and the spiritual world.[2]

ART IN CONTEXT

THE KUBA NGAADY MWAASH AND YORUBA (pronounced YORubah) Aroni (pronounced AROHnee) masks in this lesson represent two very different styles of mask making. The former is geometric (characterized by lines, shapes, and patterns). Its surface is made from an assortment of materials—copper tacks, plant fiber, beads, shells, cotton, and raffia. In contrast, the Aroni mask is volumetric (emphasizing three-dimensional form). Unlike the Kuba mask, which is covered with many decorative elements, Aroni's surface was once covered with a single material—bright, multicolored paint. When seen in performance, the arrangement of the elements of art—color, line, shape, texture, space—provide clues to the masks' identity and character.

The Kuba people live along the Sankuru River in the Democratic Republic of the Congo. The kingdom comprises more than 10 ethnic groups united under a single king.[3] The history and origin stories of the Kuba people play a key role in the Ngaady Mwaash performance.

Although the delicately featured Ngaady Mwaash has an elaborate combination of materials and patterns, visual order is maintained through their symmetrical arrangement. The harmony and balance of the composition reflect the beauty and comportment essential to Mweel's role as first queen of the Kuba kingdom. An observer described her graceful and stately dance:

Her performance style is sensuous as the body, legs, arms, and hands of the dancer move in fluid gestures…. [that are] accentuated with the use of a flywhisk held in one hand. The long skirt and overskirt worn by the Ngady Mwaash masked dancers prohibit the flamboyant torso and leg movement characteristic of male masquerade performances."[4]

Ngaady Mwaash appears primarily in masquerades performed at funerals of initiated men, ceremonies for dignitaries, and male initiation rites, all of which commemorate the creation of the Kuba kingdom. Ngaady Mwaash never appears alone but with one of two male masked figures. One of these figures may be the powerful king Woot (pronounced wote), said to be Mweel's brother and husband. Their relationship created the first man and woman from whom all Kuba royalty descends. The other figure with whom she may appear is Bwoom (pronounced bwohm), a man from the surrounding forest, who opposes Woot's authority and vies for Mweel's attention. As with most African masquerades, a man performs the part of Ngaady Mwaash.

RELATED ARTWORK

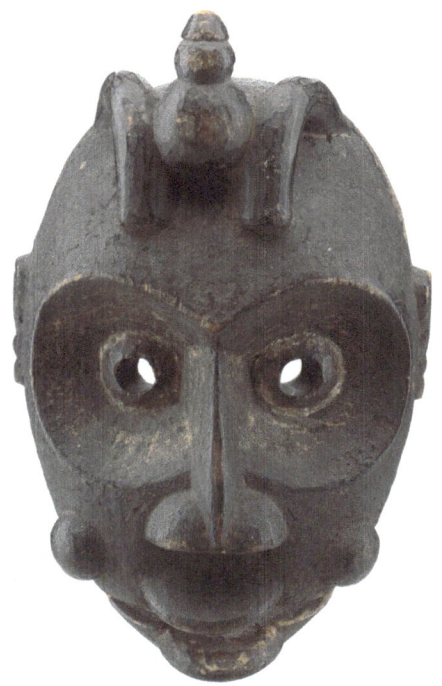

UNLIKE THE HIGHLY DECORATED and relatively flat Ngaady Mwaash, the Aroni mask of the Yoruba people was carved of wood in a series of curved lines and rounded, repeated forms. Aroni's volumetric, dome-like cheeks contrast with its concave, sunken eye sockets. The form of its tubular curved horns is repeated in the shape of the ears. The bridge of the nose and the nostrils are prominently ridged. Instead of the soft melding of one form into the next as seen on the Kuba mask, planes on the Aroni mask meet abruptly in ridges formed by obtuse and acute angles. In its original state, Aroni would have been brightly painted. Here, just a little pink is visible on the tongue that protrudes from the hinged jaw. The combination of forms are intended to evoke the face of a monkey, an apt association since Aroni is a trickster forest spirit.

On Aroni's forehead, a spherical calabash gourd called an "ado" holds magical medicines that the capricious spirit can use in a number of ways. Before entering the forest, hunters ask Aroni to make the chase fruitful. But, Aroni is unpredictable. He may use the potion to help huntsmen find prey, or he may, on a whim, trick them and use it to make hunters lose their way and vanish.

Honoring the ancestors, Aroni performs in annual celebrations with a suite of masks that include animal spirits—snakes, hyenas, lions, rams, insects, and monkeys, among others—as well as human entities, such as husbands and wives, people drunk on alcohol, foreigners, and

TRICKSTER MASK (ARONI)
Early 20th century

Artist Unidentified
Yoruba region, probably Oyo, Nigeria
Wood, encrustation, and plant fiber
Purchase with Exchange of Funds from Gift of Mr. and Mrs. Joseph Gerofsky; Gift of Irene Gulck; Gift of Mr. and Mrs. Alan Meyers; Gift of Dr. Joseph H. Seipp, Jr.; and Gift of Alan Wurtzburger, BMA 1983.83

mothers of twins. The elaborate masquerade is highly interactive and humorous as spirits and entities appear without warning.

> [Sometimes maskers] set up a large encircling mat wall (that sometimes dances by itself) in the center of the performance space. At the most appropriate dramatic moment, the mat wall will collapse to reveal a miracle like a fish or crocodile with snapping, gaping jaws…. Monkey masquerader[s] jump down out of trees or from rooftops…. Masked attendants escort [Aroni] about the performance area while drummers play rhythms associated with songs for Aroni and audience members give alms and sometimes come forward to seek blessings.[5]

Yoruba lore suggests that Aroni has only one arm and one leg. The masker communicates these physical aspects by performing with an arm behind his back. He may also hop up and down with his legs together in a tight cylindrical costume or lean on a staff and move in a way that suggests he has only one leg.[6] Aroni's elaborate costume often includes natural materials that allude to the forest in which the spirit dwells. One observer noted that rough burlap costumes were painted green and decorated with roots, leaves, and vines.[7]

Aroni's wild and unpredictable nature can only be communicated through a combination of mask, costume, and performance. His dramatically painted, monkey-like face; a costume that exaggerates his physical characteristics; and a masquerade that is both energetic and erratic must all be present to tell the tale of the forest spirit.

The Yoruba are a collection of kingdoms in southwest Nigeria and Bénin. The Oyo kingdom, in which the BMA Aroni mask was probably made, is part of the Yoruba. The kingdoms have numerous densely populated urban areas that support a market economy. In each urban center or town, a council of chiefs usually assists a traditional leader in decision making.[8]

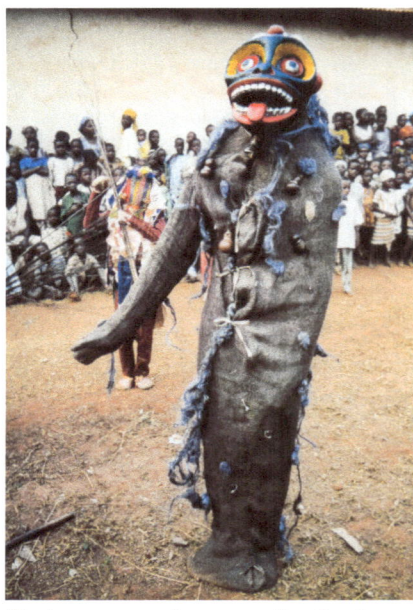

Yoruba masquerade representing Aroni. Egbada, Yoruba, Nigeria.

Photo: Henry John Drewal, 1978. Courtesy of the Henry John and Margaret Thompson Drewal Collection. Eliot Eliston Photographic Archive, National Museum of African Art, Smithsonian Institution.

[1] Katie Dowling, *Arts of Africa* (Chicago: The Art Institute of Chicago, 1998), 63.

[2] David A. Binkley, "Ideology of Male and Female Movement: A Kuba Mask (Ngady Mwaash)," in *See the Music Hear the Dance*, ed. Frederick John Lamp (Munich: Prestel Publishing, 2004), 172.

[3] "Kuba," University of Iowa Museum of Art, accessed January 16, 2015, http://africa.uima.uiowa.edu/peoples/show/Kuba.

[4] Binkley, "Ideology of Male and Female Movement," 173.

[5] Henry John Drewal, "A Spectacle of Miracles: The Yoruba Forest Spirit Mask (Aroni)," in *See the Music Hear the Dance*, ed. Frederick John Lamp (Munich: Prestel Publishing, 2004), 145.

[6] Marilyn Hammersley Houlberg, "Notes on Egungun Masquerades Among the Oyo Yoruba," *African Arts* 11, 3 (April, 1978), 61.

[7] Drewal, "A Spectacle of Miracles," 145.

[8] "Yoruba," University of Iowa Museum of Art, accessed January 16, 2015, http://africa.uima.uiowa.edu/peoples/show/Yoruba.

CLASSROOM ACTIVITIES

ACTIVITY 1:
Comparing and Contrasting Geometrics and Volumetrics
Grades: K–2, 3–5
Subjects: English Language Arts, Visual Arts

Students will look closely at the Female Mask and the Trickster Mask and describe the two artworks. Using the following questions, students will explore the similarities and differences between the two objects in a class discussion. The teacher will record student responses in a Venn diagram on a black/white board.

- What colors do you see?
- What shapes do you see?
- What textures do you see?
- What forms do you see?
- What materials do you think these artworks might be made from?

As students offer responses, the teacher will share contextual information about the objects, explaining that Yoruba art favors volume while Kuba art emphasizes geometry. The teacher will then introduce the terms "geometric," meaning the geometric elements of lines and shapes (such as circles and squares), and "volumetric," meaning elements that take up three-dimensional space (such as cubes and orbs).

The teacher will divide students into pairs and ask them to identify the geometric elements of the Kuba mask and the volumetric elements of the Yoruba mask. Teacher will then invite student pairs to share their observations.

To extend this activity, student pairs can be given several images of other artworks, either from this resource or from other resources, such as the BMA collections page at https://artbma.org/collections/index.html. The student pairs can discuss whether they think certain artworks are more geometric or volumetric, supporting their assertions with examples from the images. The teacher will then invite student pairs to share examples of how they categorized certain artworks for class discussion.

ACTIVITY 2:
Exploring the West African Trickster Character in Art and Literature
Grades: 3–5
Subjects: English Language Arts, Visual Arts

Students will examine the Trickster Mask and each write down at least five descriptive words. The teacher will then ask the following questions to guide the discussion, recording responses on a black/white board.

- What colors do you see?
- What shapes do you see?
- What textures do you see?
- What forms do you see?
- What materials do you think these artworks might be made from?

As students share their responses, the teacher will note relevant information about the context and meaning of the object, explaining that the mask was intended to depict Aroni, a spiritual entity from the Yoruba region in Nigeria. They can also share the contextual photo from this resource that shows Aroni in performance, with a full costume and brightly painted mask (as the Trickster Mask would have originally appeared).

The teacher will then read an illustrated West African trickster story, such as one focused on Anansi, the spider trickster, as told by the Ashanti people of Ghana. (Anansi is linked to wisdom, folktales, and linguistic talent and is most often associated with oral narratives.) After students listen to the story, the teacher will divide them into groups of four and ask them to discuss the trickster using the following questions.

- What does it mean to trick someone? When can it be good and when can it be bad?
- How does the trickster actually trick other characters?
- What does this say about the trickster?
- What does this say about the other characters in the story?
- What lessons can be learned from this trickster story?
- What connections to your life can you find in the story?

After group discussion, the teacher will ask all students to share their responses to the questions above. Each student will write a one- to two-paragraph text explaining his/her understanding of the West African trickster using evidence from the discussion of the object and the illustrated book.

STANDARDS AND CURRICULUM

COMMON CORE STATE STANDARDS

English Language Arts

Grade 1
CCSS.ELA-Literacy.SL.1.1. Participate in collaborative conversations with diverse partners about grade 1 topics and texts with peers and adults in small and larger groups.

CCSS.ELA-Literacy.W.1.2. Write informative/ explanatory texts in which they name a topic, supply some facts about the topic, and provide some sense of closure.

Grade 2
CCSS.ELA-Literacy.SL.2.1. Participate in collaborative conversations with diverse partners about grade 2 topics and texts with peers and adults in small and larger groups.

CCSS.ELA-Literacy.W.2.2. Write informative/ explanatory texts in which they introduce a topic, use facts and definitions to develop points, and provide a concluding statement or section.

Grade 3
CCSS.ELA-Literacy.SL.3.1. Engage effectively in a range of collaborative discussions (one-on-one, in groups, and teacher-led) with diverse partners on grade 3 topics and texts, building on others' ideas and expressing their own clearly.

CCSS.ELA-Literacy.W.3.2. Write informative/ explanatory texts to examine a topic and convey ideas and information clearly.

MARYLAND STATE CURRICULUM

Visual Arts

Grade 1
1.2.b. Use color, line, shape, texture, and form to represent ideas visually from observation, memory, and imagination.
1.3.a. Explore and discuss the qualities of color, line, shape, texture, and form in artworks.
2.1.a. Observe works of art and identify ways that artists express ideas about people, places, and events.

Grade 2
1.1.a. Describe colors, lines, shapes, textures, forms, and space found in observed objects and the environment.
1.2.a. Describe how artists use color, line, shape, texture, form, and space to represent ideas visually from observation, memory, and imagination.
2.1.a. Observe works of art and describe how artists express ideas about people, places, and events.
2.2.b. Communicate a variety of reasons for creating artworks, such as feelings, experiences, events, places, and ideas.

Grade 3
1.1.a. Describe similarities and differences between the elements of art in observed forms.
1.2.a. Compare and describe how artists communicate what they see, know, feel, and imagine using art vocabulary.
1.2.b. Represent ideas and feelings visually that describe what is seen, felt, known, and imagined.
1.3.a. Describe how the elements of art and principles of design are organized to communicate personal meaning in visual compositions.
2.2.a. Discuss and compare how selected artworks from different times or cultures are similar or different (e.g. common themes, content, form, and style).

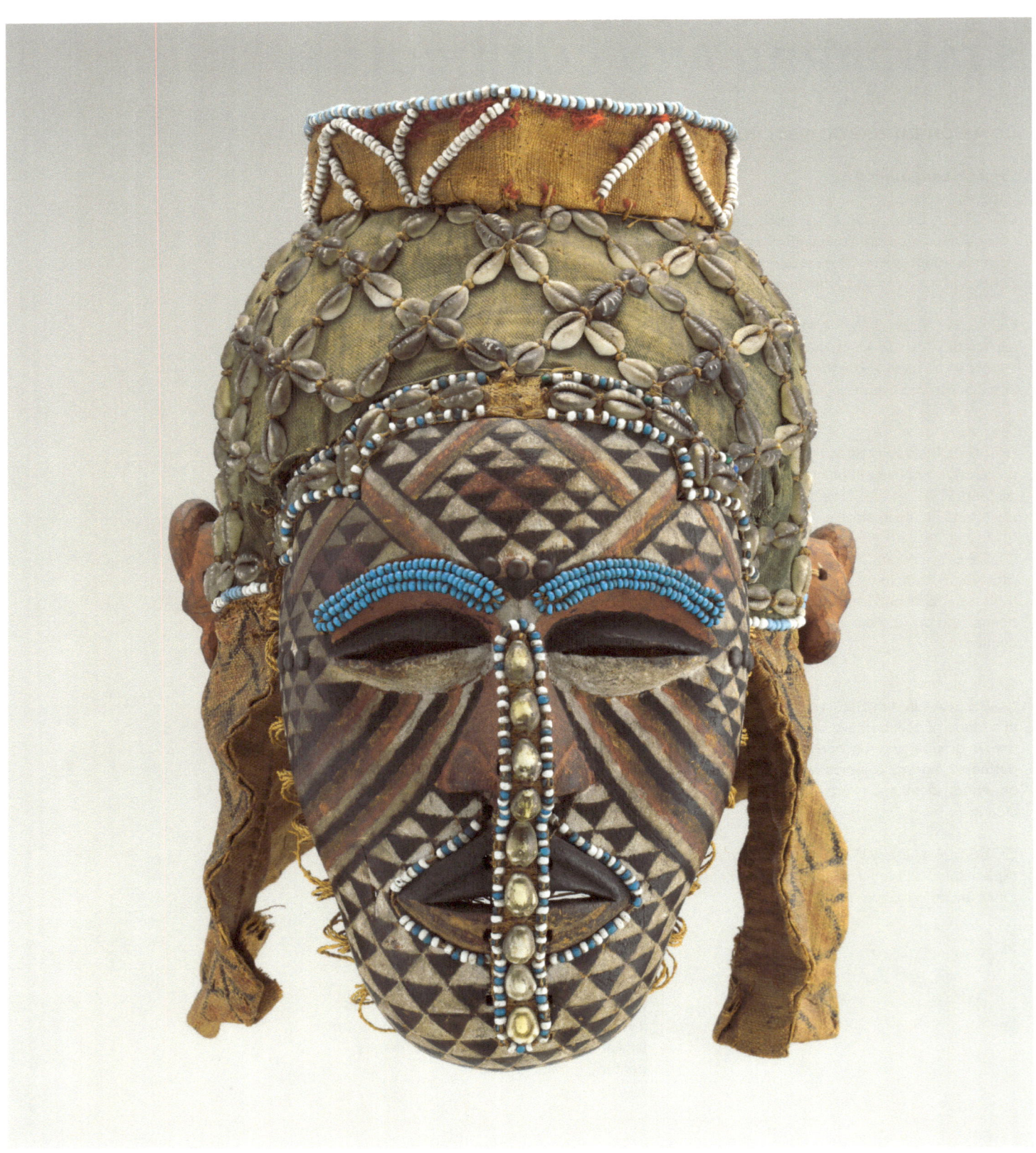

Female Mask (Ngaady Mwaash). Late 19th–early 20th century. Kuba kingdom, Democratic Republic of the Congo. Wood, cloth, copper alloy tacks, plant fibers, cowrie shells, glass beads, and paint. Gift of Alan Wurtzburger, BMA 1954.145.77

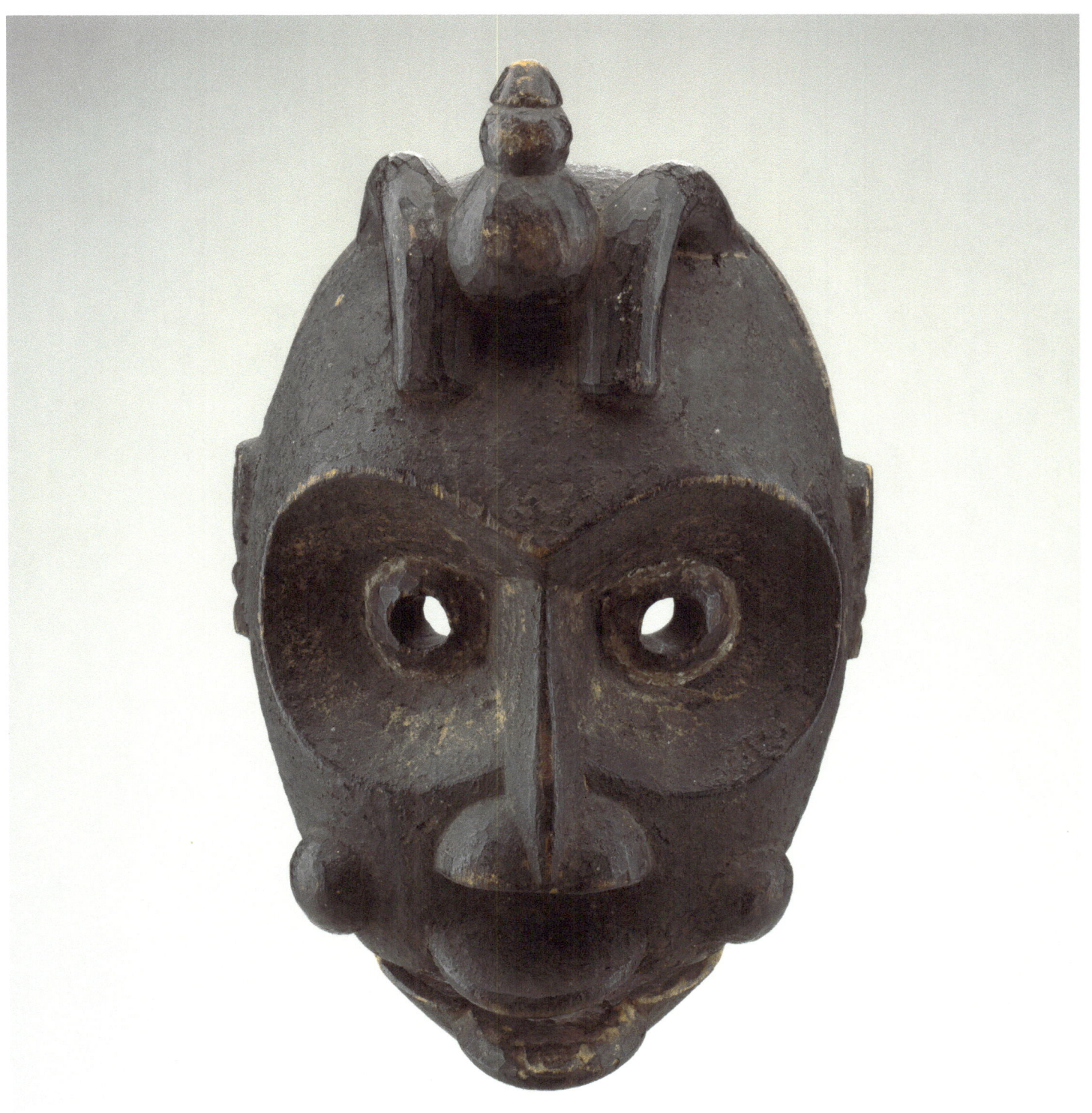

Trickster Mask (Aroni). Early 20th century. Yoruba region, probably Oyo kingdom, Nigeria. Wood, encrustation, plant fiber. Purchase with exchange funds from Gift of Mr. and Mrs. Joseph Gerofsky; Gift of Irene Gulck; Gift of Mr. and Mrs. Alan Meyers; Gift of Dr. Joseph H. Seipp, Jr.; and Gift of Alan Wurtzburger, BMA 1983.83

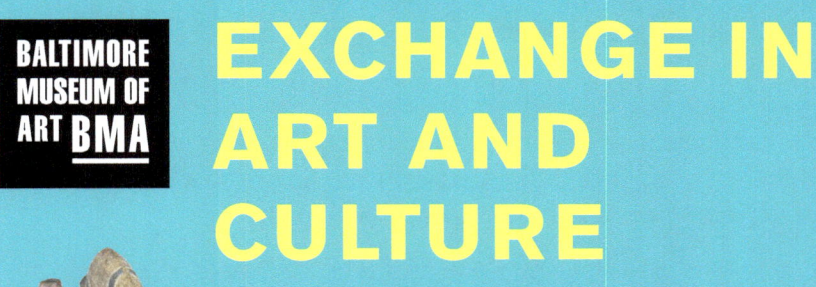

EXCHANGE IN ART AND CULTURE

KEY TERMS
- Colonial Rule
- Composite
- Gold
- Islam
- Trade

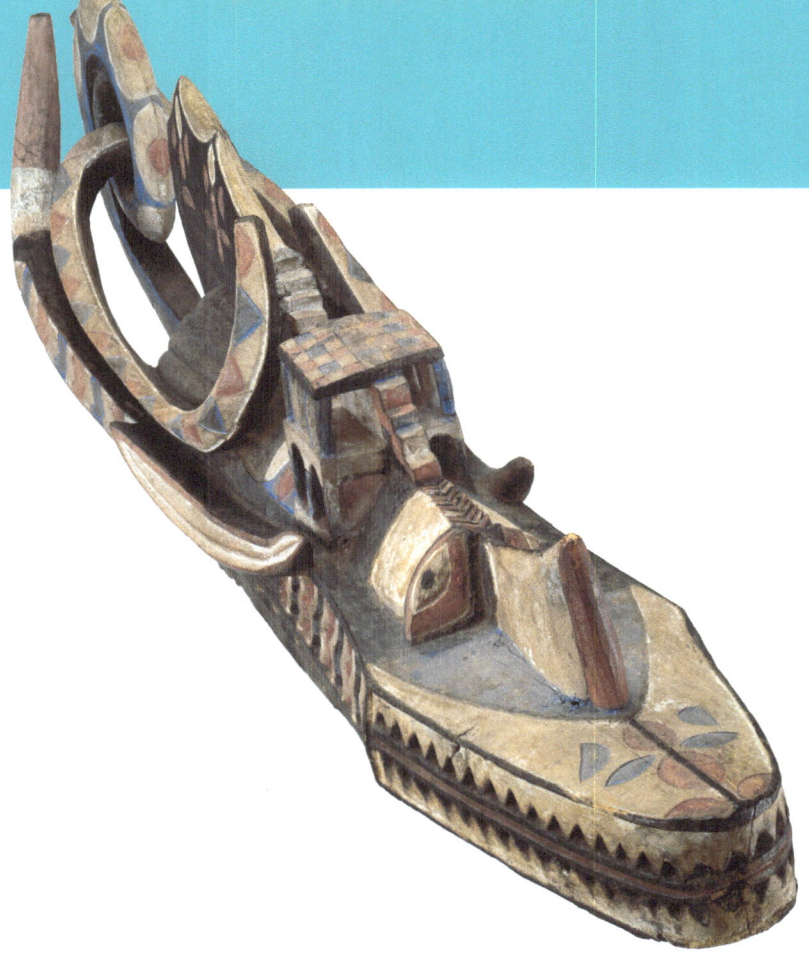

HEADDRESS (BANDA OR KUMBADUBA) Early 20th century

Artist Unidentified
Baga or Nalu region, Guinea or Guinea-Bissau
Wood, pigment, and iron
Partial gift of Valerie Franklin, Los Angeles, and
Purchase with Exchange Funds Provided by
Twenty-Seven Donors, BMA 1990.2

CLOSE LOOKING

THE BANDA (pronounced BAHNdah), meaning "Composite Human Beast," made by a Baga (pronounced BAHgah) carver, is a fusion of human and animal forms. Carved from a single piece of wood, its human features include a nose, eyes, scarification marks on the face, and a woman's braided hairstyle that is visible between the eyes and again above the head. The headdress is also decorated with a crocodile jaw and a chameleon tail, antelope horns, and the body of a snake. Each element is painted with a unique design of blue, white, and red to harmonize the disparate parts. The headdress itself is in the shape of a canoe and is, perhaps, a reference to the location of the Baga along the Atlantic Coast of Guinea and Guinea-Bissau. In the center of the headdress, the presence of a two-story Roman Catholic church with

Baga or Nalu region, Guinea or Guinea-Bissau

stairs and colonnades—like those built by European missionaries in the 19th century—speaks to the Christian institutions that arrived in this part of Africa before and during colonial rule.

ART IN CONTEXT

CULTURES ARE NEVER STATIC. Religious conversion, trade, conflict, and migration are just some of the ways in which cultural and artistic changes arise. Sometime before the 15th century, the Baga, meaning "people of the seaside" in the Susu language, migrated from the interior highlands of Guinea to the geographically isolated lowlands of the Guinean coast.[1] This migration was made to avoid conflict with the Muslim Fulbe people (although some Baga did convert to Islam). Christian missionaries arrived in the fifteenth century shortly after Portugal began to trade with the people of coastal Guinea began.[2] Written sources beginning in the mid-17th century tell of the building of churches, the presence of priests, and Christian conversions in the area.[3] Catholic beliefs, represented by the ecclesiastical building on the Banda headdress, were then incorporated into existing Baga cosmology.

Banda was used to entertain senior men at meetings between villages and to protect the Baga from animal attacks and malicious spirits around the time of male initiation rites.[4] The various elements on the headdress harness and utilize their sources, combined spiritual power to ward off malevolence. The headdress could evoke the strength of the crocodile or ward off its attack. It summoned the antelope for an easy hunt or to give a hunter antelope-like speed while hunting. Perhaps the inclusion of the church acted as a talisman as well. Together, the Banda's visual elements suggest the complex relationship between the Baga and the earthly and spiritual worlds.

A large raffia cape attached to the underside of the Banda headdress covered the masker from his face to his knees. Loose pants with ruffles of raffia at the bottom and a short cloth cape around the back of the costume completed the outfit.[5] More than five feet long and very heavy, the mask in performance required extraordinary athleticism on the part of the performer. Not only is the mask very heavy, but the choreography depicted a large number of animals, including a powerful bull and a bird diving for fish in the sea. Below, art historian Frederick Lamp describes one part of a performance he witnessed in 1987 in which a bird was evoked by the masker:

> Like a predatory bird fishing, [the dancer] takes high steps, then lunges the headdress downward… crouching low, he puts his snout to the ground, shudders, and makes pecking motions toward the ground, then points the headdress high in the air, like the bird swallowing its fish. As a bird in flight, he circles around the space, tilting the headdress toward the spectators and flinging out the raffia with his hands, prancing with bent knees.[6]

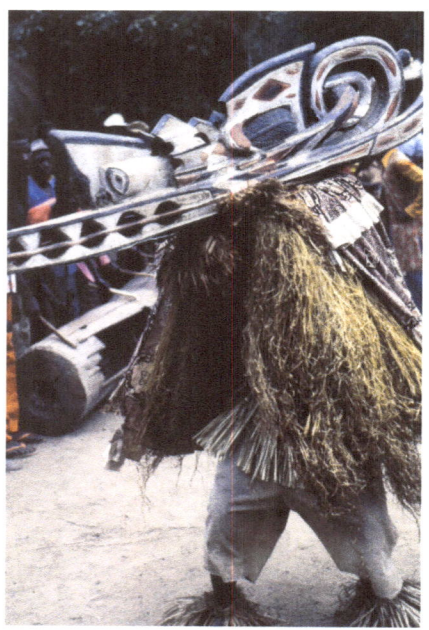

Banda Dance. Baga Mandon, Guinea.
Photo: Frederick John Lamp, 1987

At various points in the frenetic performance, the masker, always a young man, would crouch down and then jump up, lifting Banda high over his head. He would spin, then make multiple figure eights before plunging the headdress close to the ground. The performance would last for several hours. When one masker would tire, another male initiate would step in.

After Guinean independence from French colonial rule in 1958 and during the subsequent Marxist regime, many aspects of Baga culture were prohibited and religious objects destroyed. When the regime fell in 1984, Baga cultural expressions experienced a rebirth, including the reintroduction of Banda. Today, however, the headdress is masqueraded only for village and visitor entertainment.[7]

RELATED ARTWORK

FOR APPROXIMATELY 500 YEARS, beginning around 1400, the Akan of southern Ghana and the Côte d'Ivoire used gold dust mined from their river beds and forests as currency.[8] The commodity was much desired and made the Akan (pronounced ahCAHN) a valuable partner to both North African traders who crossed the Sahara desert and European merchants on West Africa's coast. The Akan lacked salt, an element necessary to basic health. People in North Africa could easily mine salt; conversely, the Akan could easily mine gold, and a long distance trade route was thus established. North African traders carried bars of salt, cloth, tobacco, and tools to trading centers on the Niger River. The Akan traded for these goods using gold, ivory, kola nuts, pepper, and sugar, as well as enslaved people.[9] In addition, the Akan traded with European merchants on the Ghanaian coast, exchanging gold for guns and gunpowder, tools, paper, cloth and clothing, livestock, fruit, tobacco, sugar cane, eyeglasses, and glass beads.[10]

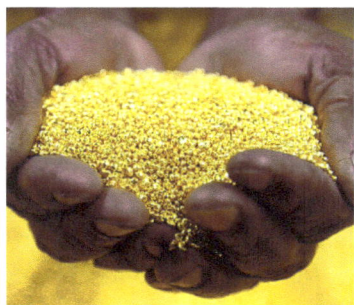

A handful of gold dust

The Akan and their trading partners used a system of brass weights and scales to determine the price of goods. Both buyer and seller brought their own weights and scale to the negotiation. An Akan tradesman, hoping to get top price for his goods, presented a heavy weight. Wanting to pay less than asking price, the buyer presented a lighter one. Negotiations continued until they agreed on which combination of weights determined the amount of gold dust to be paid for salt or another commodity. Once a price was set, the buyer measured gold dust on the scale until the weight balanced. The trader then reweighed the gold with his system to ensure the deal was equitable.[11]

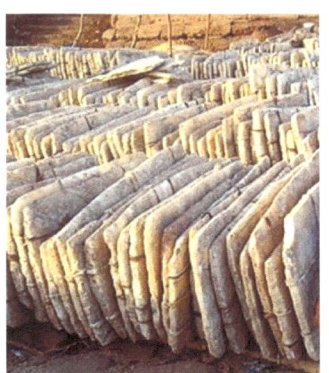

Salt blocks ready to be traded for gold
Photo: Dan Heller

From 1400–1900, Akan metalworkers made millions of weights that were commissioned by Akan people and various trading partners.

Weights were made in multiple series, one of which was based on the European ounce and another on Arabic measurements for North African trade. The weights themselves are of two types, the first abstract and geometric and the second figural or representative of everyday objects. The BMA has a collection of more than 650 Akan weights, some in the shapes of fish, snakes, birds, turtles, and scorpions. This weight in the form of two sandals may represent those removed by Muslim worshippers prior to prayer. It is through the North African trade routes that Islam spread across the Sahara desert southwest and into southern Ghana and the Côte d'Ivoire.

For information on the Akan lost-wax casting process (used in the late 20th century for casting different kinds of brass objects), see "Akan Brass Casting" in the online resource "Art & Life in Africa" from the University of Iowa: http://africa.uima.uiowa.edu/topic-essays/show/27.

For a further exploration of gold weights, teachers and students can refer to the February 2015 issue of Art-To-Go, "Super-small Sculptures from Africa": https://artbma.org/documents/atg/pdf/ATG_2-15.pdf. They can also visit the collections page of the BMA to search for other gold weights at the Museum. (Use the term "Abrammuo" for the best results.) https://artbma.org/collections/african.html.

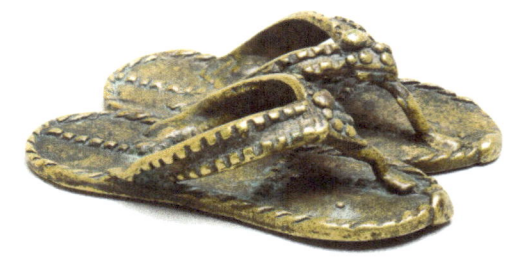

GOLD-DUST WEIGHT (ABRAMMUO)
1700–1900

Artist Unidentified
Akan region, Ghana or Côte d'Ivoire
Brass
Gift of Helen 'Muffie' Lippincott McElhiney,
BMA 1988.1205

THE ECONOMY OF THE HISTORICALLY nomadic Tuareg (pronounced TWAreg) people is based on trade, livestock, and agriculture. Their trade routes extended from the northern Mediterranean coasts of Algeria and Libya to Mali and Niger along the southern edge of the Sahara desert.[12] Using camel caravans, Tuareg merchants brought goods such as dates, millet, salt, clothes, leather products, and ostrich feathers to the northern coasts, and from there they were traded throughout the world.[13]

The vast majority of Tuareg are Muslim. Soon after the prophet Muhammad's death in 632, Muslim warriors swept from Egypt to Morocco and then south, converting many ethnic groups to Islam.[14] Over the course of several centuries, Islam continued to establish a strong presence in these regions and by the 11th century, many people had converted. A wealthy Muslim Tuareg merchant would have wanted to carry the Koran, the central religious text of Islam, with him on caravans. Containers like the one in the BMA collection allowed for the Koran's safe transport. The box would have been worn on a cord around the owner's neck. Messages in Arabic decorate the case, saying, "It is Allah who sustains the heavens and the earth" and, repeating the first words of the Koran, "In the name of Allah, the Merciful, the Compassionate." Each letter of the inscriptions is aligned differently, so that the devotee would contemplate its form in order to decode its message. The metal's shine is a metaphor for the light of God's word as told in the Koran.

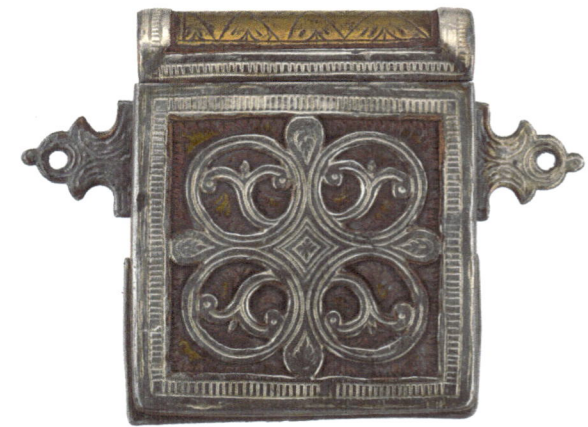

CONTAINER FOR A KORAN
Early 20th century

Artist Unidentified
Tuareg areas of Niger, Algeria, or Mali
Copper alloy, nickel, and lead
Anonymous Gift, BMA 2002.142

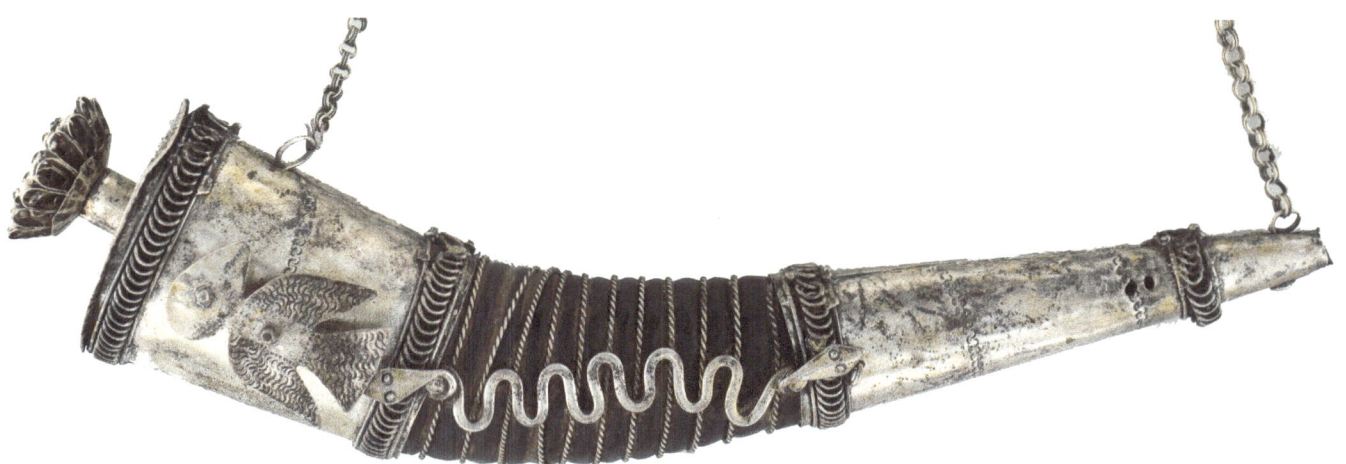

THE FON KINGDOM OF SIERRA LEONE amassed great wealth between the early 18th and mid-19th centuries by conquering coastal states and monopolizing the region's trade in enslaved people with Europe.[15] Upon taking people captive, the nobility singled out artists and retained them to ensure constant innovation in the arts.

This personal ornament in the shape of a gunpowder horn is purely ornamental. It cannot hold powder, because the lid does not open. The object is decorated with filigree, ornate ornamental work made of thin wire formed into delicate shapes. The rosette on the "lid" of the horn is finely formed, and decoration continues with a bird and two-headed snake on one side. The object reflects the artist's familiarity with European Victorian jewelry which is often highly embellished. The Victorian filigree work and gunpowder horn shape are both derived from European antecedents. In this example, silver covers an actual antelope horn.

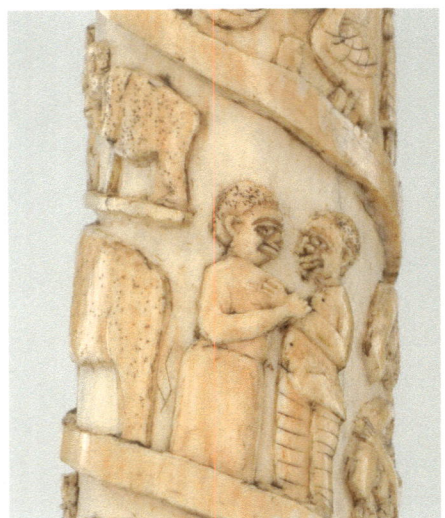
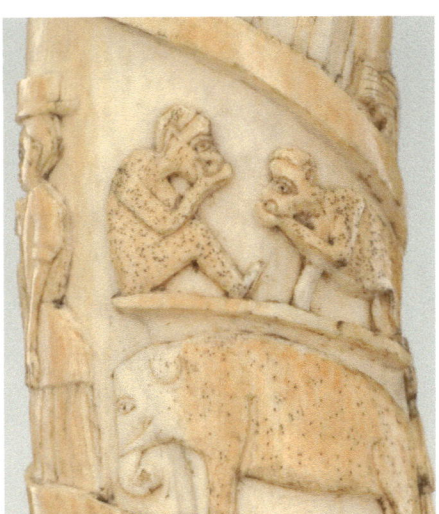
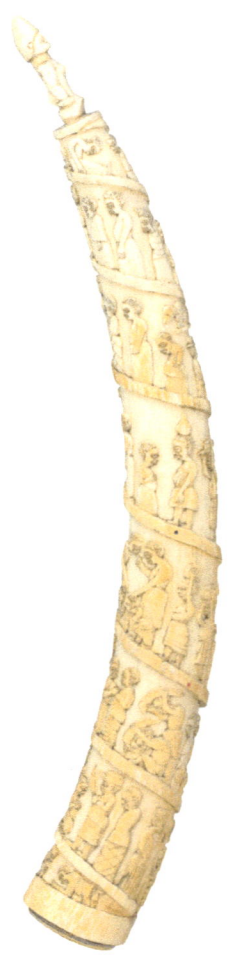

KONGO (pronounced KONgo) kingdom sculptors of the Loango coast in Democratic Republic of the Congo sold carved souvenir tusks to European traders and officials, beginning with the Portuguese in the 16th century.[16] The images around the BMA tusk depict scenes of merchants trading and African porters carrying heavy boxes and ivory under the watchful eye of European colonials. Figures of African people in traditional dress, African people in European dress, and white Europeans reflect the rigid strata of colonial enforced labor. The spiral composition reflects the Kongo belief that life is a cycle of birth, life, death, and rebirth. More than one thousand similar tusks were sold at the peak of the ivory trade in the mid- to late-19th century.

TUSK CARVED IN RELIEF
Late 19th–early 20th century

Artist Unidentified
Kongo kingdom, Democratic Republic of the Congo or Angola
Elephant ivory
Gift of Alan Wurtzburger, BMA 1953.133a

1 Bruce L. Mouser, "Who and Where Were the Baga?: European Perceptions from 1793 to 1821," *History in Africa*, 29 (2002): 337.

2 Lamp, *The Art of the Baga*, 35.

3 Lamp, *The Art of the Baga*, 37.

4 "Mask (Banda)," The Metropolitan Museum of Art, accessed January 30, 2015, http://www.metmuseum.org/toah/works-of-art/1978.412.307.

5 Frederick John Lamp, *The Art of the Baga*, 146.

6 Frederick John Lamp, *The Art of the Baga*, 148.

7 "Mask (Banda)," The Metropolitan Museum of Art, accessed January 30, 2015, http://www.metmuseum.org/toah/works-of-art/1978.412.307.

8 John Picton, "West Africa and the Guinea Coast," in *Africa the Art of a Continent*, ed. Tom Phillips (Munich: Prestel Verlag, 1999), 442.

9 "What is Currency? Lessons from Historic Africa," *Smithsonian in Your Classroom*, May/June 1998, 3.

10 "What is Currency? Lessons from Historic Africa," 5.

11 "What is Currency? Lessons from Historic Africa," 4.

12 "Islam and Islamic Arts in Africa," University of Iowa Museum of Art, accessed February 2, 2015, http://africa.uima.uiowa.edu/topic-essays/show/Islam+and+Islamic+Arts+in+Africa.

13 "Tuareg," University of Iowa Museum of Art, accessed February 2, 2015, http://africa.uima.uiowa.edu/peoples/show/Tuareg.

14 "Islam and Islamic Arts in Africa."

15 "Fon," University of Iowa Museum of Art, accessed February 2, 2015, http://africa.uima.uiowa.edu/peoples/show/Fon.

16 "Kongo Ivories," Metropolitan Museum of Art, accessed March 18, 2015, www.metmuseum.org/toah/hd/kong/hd_kong.htm.

CLASSROOM ACTIVITIES

ACTIVITY 1:
Creating a Composite
Grades: 6–8
**Subjects: English Language Arts, History/
Social Studies, Visual Arts**

Students will look closely at the Headdress (Banda or Kumbaduba) and respond to the following questions in a class discussion. The teacher will record responses on the black/white board.

- What are the art elements—color, line, shape, texture, and form—you see in the artwork?
- Are there parts of the artwork that look familiar to you? If so, what are the parts and what do they remind you of?

The teacher will share contextual information about the headdress, pointing out the various human, animal, and architectural elements that make the headdress a composite, explaining that a "composite" is something made from parts from different sources. The definition can be written on the black/white board and left up for student reference. The teacher will also share that the purpose of creating a composite headdress was to incorporate all the elements of the Baga cosmos (including elements incorporated from the Portuguese culture with whom the Baga had been in contact) to create one figure.

The teacher will explain that, for this headdress, the Baga used the composite to express spiritual ideas, but students will explore the composite in a secular way, creating a self-portrait that focuses on personal experiences, culture, and environment. Each part of the composite portrait should correspond to the parts of each student's face. The teacher will provide magazines, newspapers, flyers, and other materials with images of people, places, and things. (For the purposes of this activity, the students should be limited to those images and not use text from the collage materials.) Using these materials and paper, scissors, and glue sticks, students will create composite collage self-portraits that reflect their interests, experiences, culture, and environment. Students will then share their artistic choices with the class in a group discussion.

For another example of composites in art, explore the composite head paintings of Italian Renaissance artist Giuseppe Archimbaldo. http://www.nga.gov/exhibitions/arcimboldoinfo.shtm

ACTIVITY 2:
Researching Gold Weights and African Trade Routes
Grades: 6–8
**Subjects: English Language Arts, History/
Social Studies, Visual Arts**

Within a unit on historic African trade networks and the spread of Islam, the teacher will divide students into groups of four and display or share copies of the Gold-Dust Weight and Container for a Koran images from this resource. Each group of students will look carefully at the images, one at a time, using the questions below to guide their discussion.

- What are the art elements—color, line, shape, texture, and form—you see in the artwork?
- Is there anything about the artwork that looks familiar to you? If so, what looks familiar?

The teacher will then invite groups to share their responses, recording them on the black/white board for future reference. As students share thoughts, the teacher will offer information about the objects, explaining how the Gold-Dust Weight was used and how it illustrates the cultural exchange that occurred due to the gold dust currency along trade routes in West and North Africa. (Please note that this object dates to 1700–1900 CE, but it reflects some of the cultural contacts that developed in the use of gold dust beginning around 1400.) The teacher will also share the context for the Container for a Koran.

Though it dates from from the early 20th century, the work demonstrates the lasting effect of the spread of Islam in Mali.

Individual students will then use print and/or online resources to research objects from North and West African countries that reflect the spread of Islam.

For further information on the arts of the Islamic world, teachers may visit: http://www.metmuseum.org/learn/for-educators/publications-for-educators/art-of-the-islamic-world and students may wish to explore the Heilbrunn Timeline of Art History at the Metropolitan Museum of Art at http://www.metmuseum.org/toah/. If desired, the teacher may select objects from the timeline for students to choose among.

Students will use the questions below to guide their research. They will then write a one- to two-page essay on the object they have selected.

- What is the object?
- What are the art elements—color, line, shape, texture, and form—you see in the artwork? Please describe the object.
- What was the object made for?
- Can you find out who made the object?
- How does the object reflect aspects of art from the Islamic world, such as verses from the Koran in Arabic, decorative geometric and vegetal patterns, etc.?
- How did Islam come to the place where the object is from? When did this happen?

When students have completed their essays, the class should be divided into groups of four (they need not be the same four as in the first part of the activity). Students will share the results of their research and brainstorm with their group on additional research questions for their topic.

STANDARDS AND CURRICULUM

COMMON CORE STATE STANDARDS

English Language Arts
Grade 6
CCSS.ELA-Literacy.SL.6.1. Engage effectively in a range of collaborative discussions (one-on-one, in groups, and teacher-led) with diverse partners on grade 6 topics, texts, and issues, building on others' ideas and expressing their own clearly.

CCSS.ELA-Literacy.W.6.7. Conduct short research projects to answer a question, drawing on several sources and refocusing the inquiry when appropriate.

Grade 7
CCSS.ELA-Literacy.SL.7.1. Engage effectively in a range of collaborative discussions (one-on-one, in groups, and teacher-led) with diverse partners on grade 7 topics, texts, and issues, building on others' ideas and expressing their own clearly.

CCSS.ELA-Literacy.W.7.7. Conduct short research projects to answer a question, drawing on several sources and generating additional related, focused questions for further research and investigation.

Grade 8
CCSS.ELA-Literacy.SL.8.1. Engage effectively in a range of collaborative discussions (one-on-one, in groups, and teacher-led) with diverse partners on grade 8 topics, texts, and issues, building on others' ideas and expressing their own clearly.

CCSS.ELA-Literacy.W.8.7. Conduct short research projects to answer a question (including a self-generated question), drawing on several sources and generating additional related, focused questions that allow for multiple avenues of exploration.

MARYLAND STATE CURRICULUM

History/Social Studies
Grade 6
5.B.5.a. Describe the contributions of major African monarchies, cities, and trade networks, such as Ghana, Mali, and Songhai.
6.C.1.b. Explain how the development of transportation and communication networks influenced the movement of people, goods, and ideas from place to place, such as the trade routes in Africa, Asia, and Europe, and the spread of Islam.

Grade 7
2.A.1.a. Apply understandings of the elements of culture to the studies of modern world regions, such as art, music, religion, government, social structure, education, values, beliefs, and customs.
2.B.1.c. Analyze how cultural diffusion is influenced by factors, such as trade, migration, immigration, and conflict.

Visual Arts
Grade 6
1.3.a. Identify and describe how artists use design concepts to organize the elements of art and principles of design to convey ideas, thoughts, and feelings.
2.1.a. Compare stylistic methods used by artists of different cultures to communicate feelings, ideas, and universal themes.
2.1.b. Explain how stylistic elements that represent a historical period, social context, or culture, communicate feelings, ideas or universal themes in a visual composition.
2.2.a. Identify historical, social, and cultural themes in selected artworks that influence the beliefs, customs, or values of a society.
2.3.a. Identify subject matter, styles, and techniques representative of various cultures and periods of art history.

Grade 7
1.3.a. Compare and describe how artists use design concepts to organize the elements of art and principles of design to convey ideas, thoughts, and feelings in selected artworks.
2.1.a. Identify the roles and functions of the visual arts in expressing ideas, events, and universal themes within and among cultural groups.
2.2.a. Describe historical, social, and cultural themes in selected artworks that communicate beliefs, customs, or values of a society.
2.3.a. Describe subject matter, styles, and techniques representative of various cultures and periods of art history.

Grade 8
1.3.a. Analyze why artists may select specific design concepts to convey meaning in artistic exemplars.
2.1.a. Analyze the roles and functions of the visual arts in expressing ideas, events, and universal themes within and among cultural groups.
2.2.a. Compare historical, social, and cultural themes in selected artworks that communicate beliefs, customs, or values of a society.
2.3.a. Compare similarities and differences in subject matter, styles, and techniques among various cultures and periods of art history.

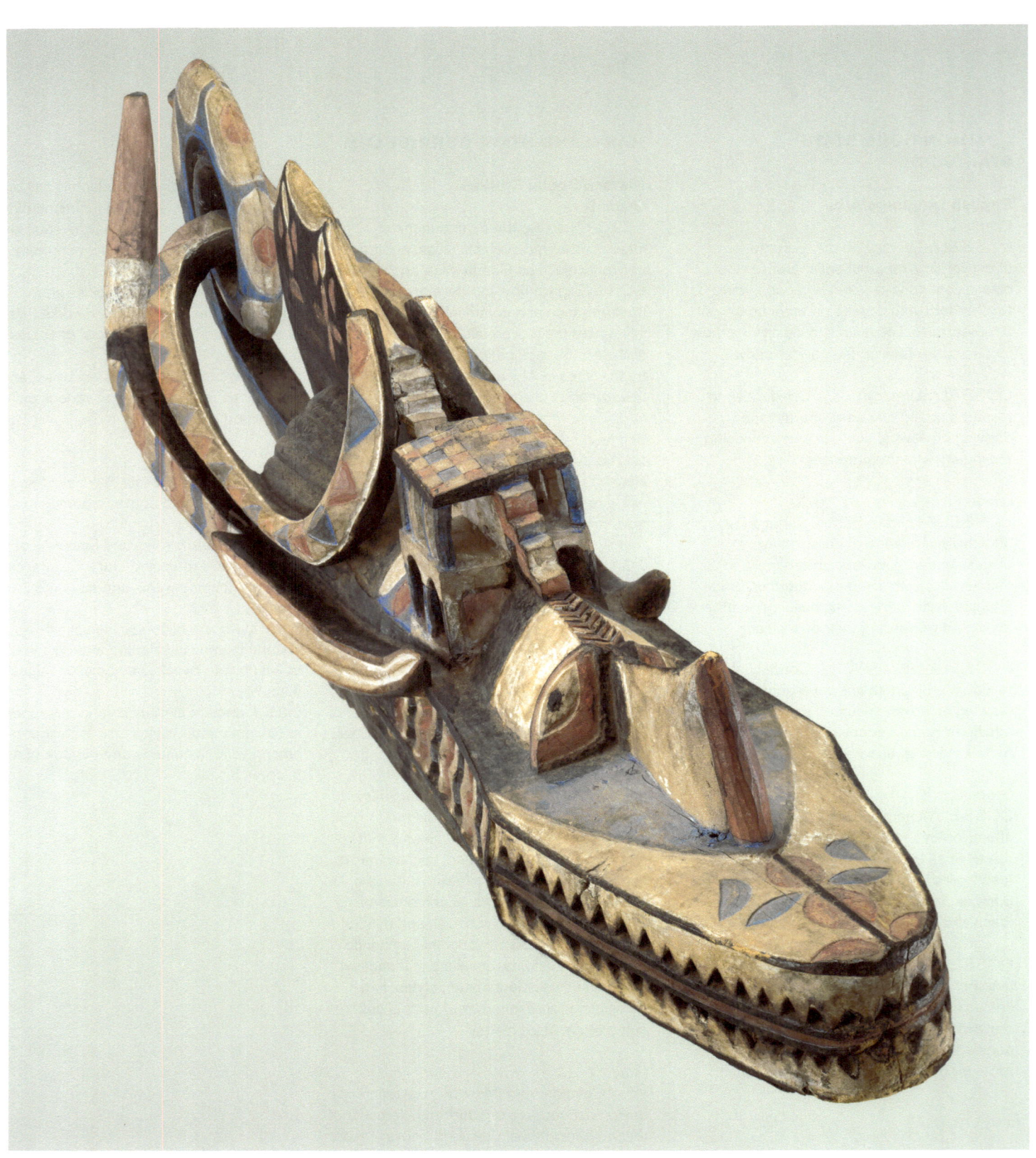

Headdress (Banda or Kumbaduba). Early 20th century. Baga or Nalu region, Guinea or Guinea-Bissau. Wood, pigment, and iron. Partial gift of Valerie Franklin, Los Angeles, and purchase with exchange funds provided by twenty-seven donors, BMA 1990.2

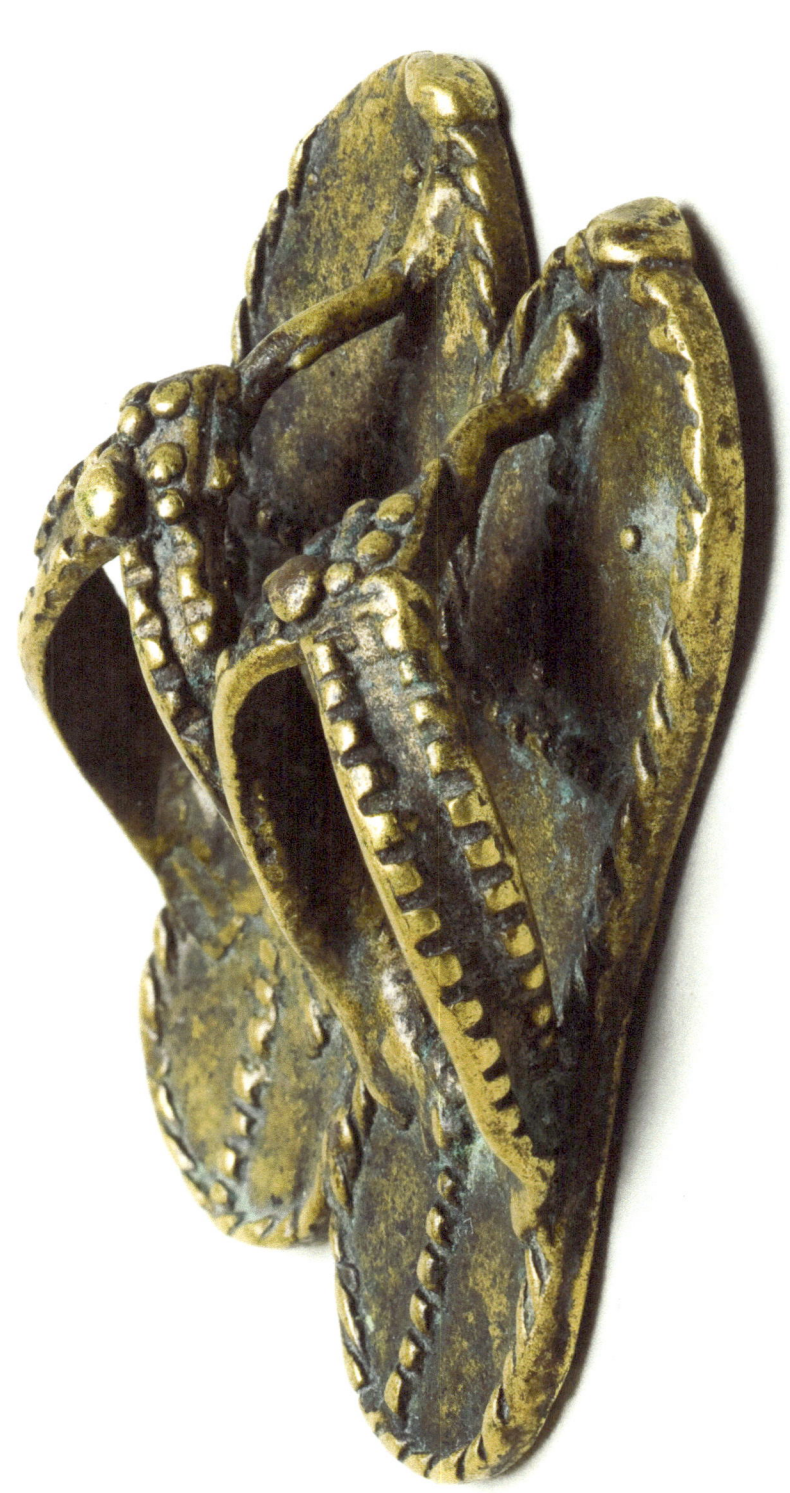

Gold-Dust Weight (Abrammuo). 1700–1900. Akan region, Ghana or Côte d'Ivoire. Brass. Gift of Helen 'Muffie' Lippincott McElhiney, Bethesda, Maryland, BMA 1988.1205

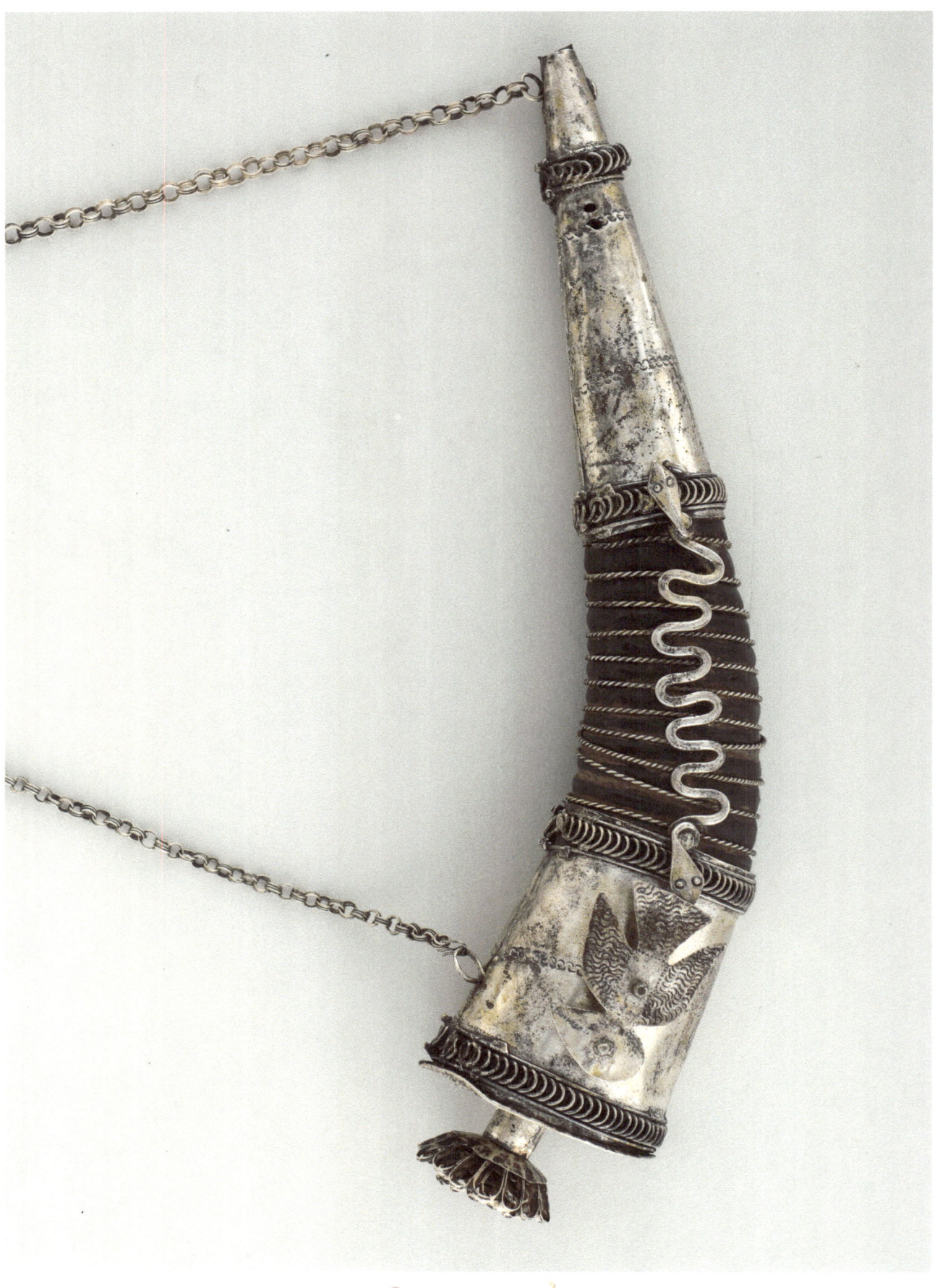

Personal Ornament. 19th–20th century. Fon kingdom of Dahomey, Benin. Silver alloy and horn. Anonymous Gift, BMA 2002.112

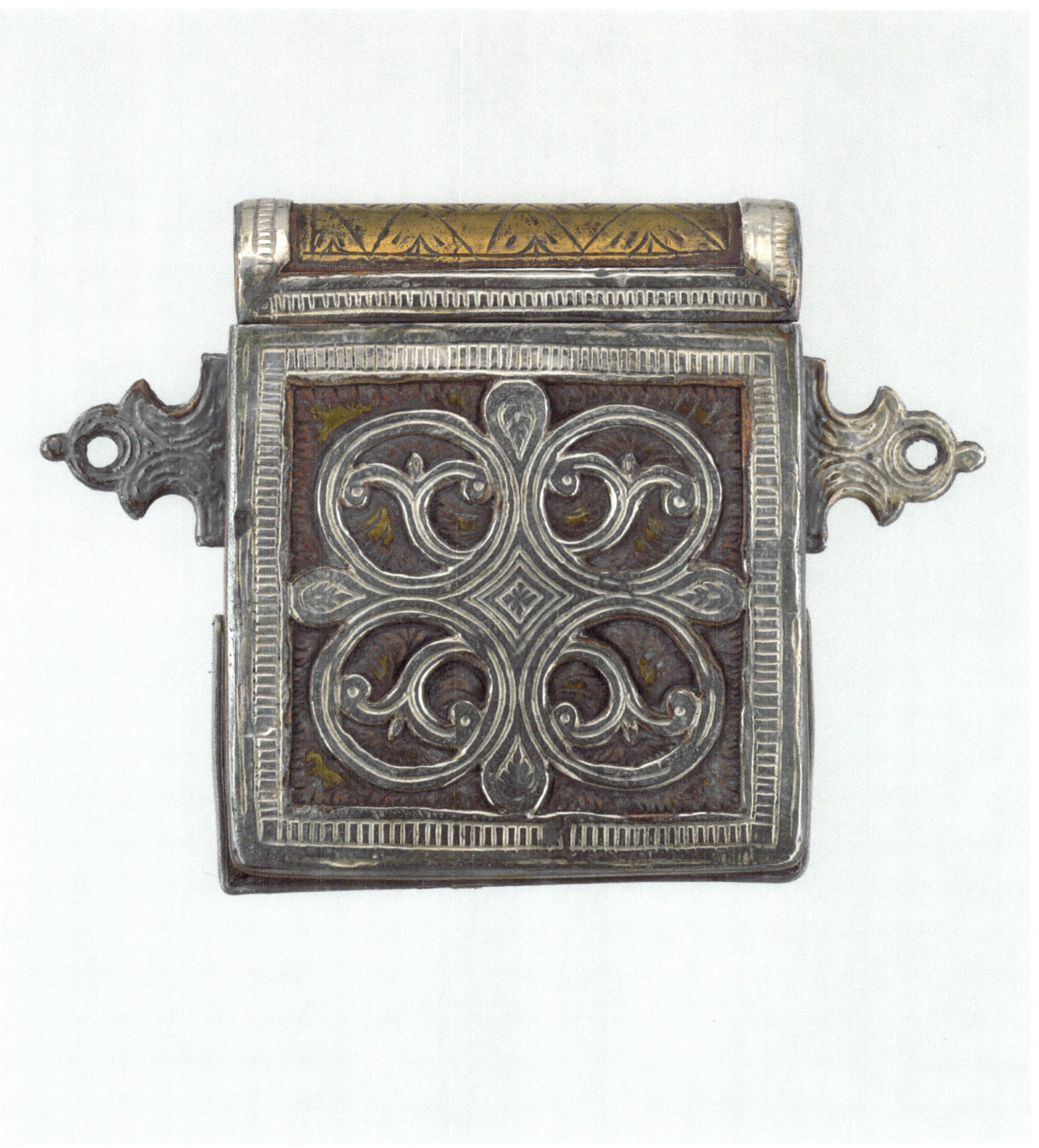

Container for a Koran. Early 20th century. Tuareg areas of Niger, Algeria, or Mali. Copper alloy, nickel, and lead. Anonymous Gift, BMA 2002.142

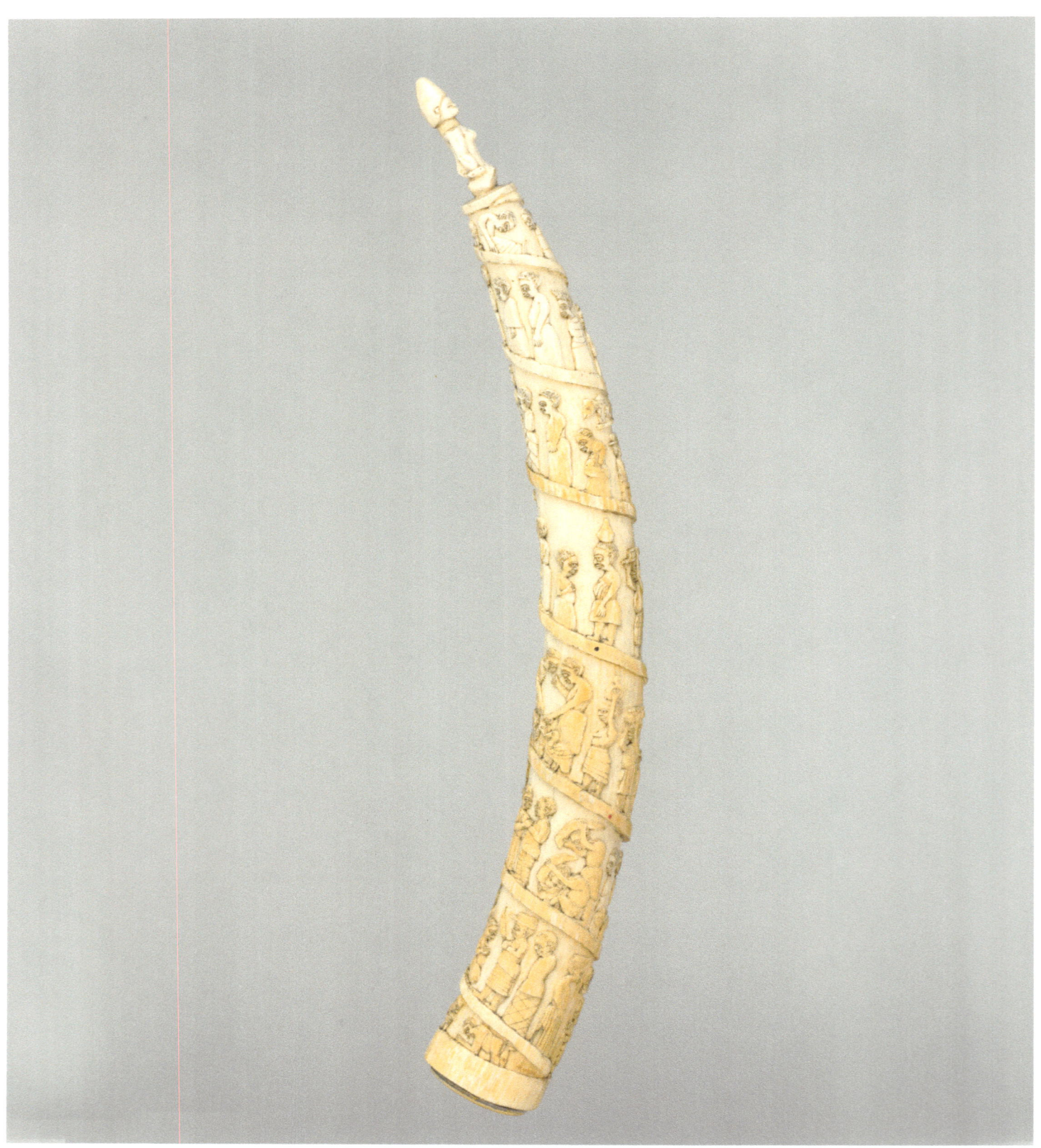

Tusk Carved in Relief. Late 19th–early 20th century. Kongo kingdom, Democratic Republic of the Congo or Angola. Elephant ivory. The Baltimore Museum of Art: Gift of Alan Wurtzburger, BMA 1953.133a

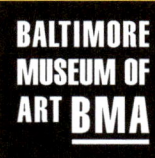

ASSERTING IDENTITY

KEY TERMS
- Apartheid
- Beadwork
- Identity
- Militia
- South Africa

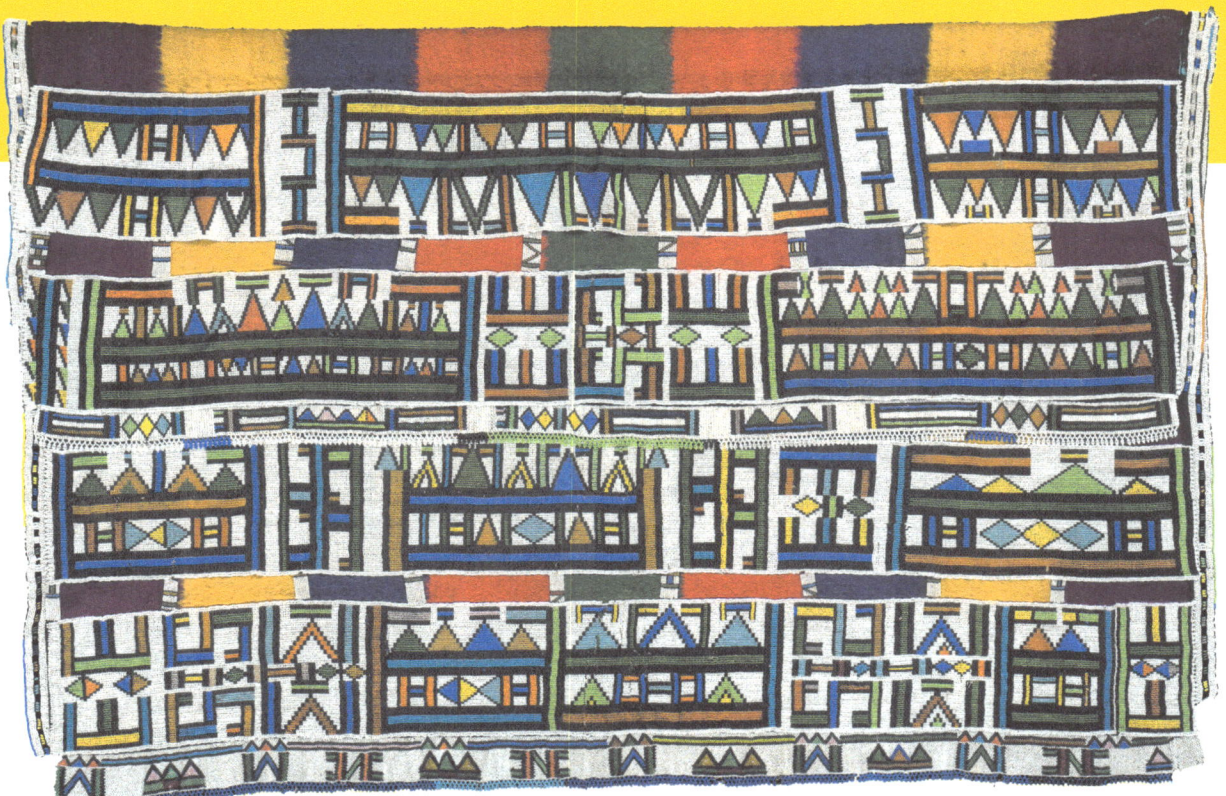

CLOSE LOOKING

THE BEADED BLANKET CAPE, sewn by an Ndebele (pronounced endeBELay) woman in South Africa around 1950, has at its base a woolen, colorfully striped Middelburg blanket of yellow, green, blue, red, and purple. The commercially made blanket is named for the town of Middelburg in the northeast region of the country, which is home to a large population of Ndebele people.

Lengths of handmade beadwork were woven separately and sewn to the blanket, with narrow widths of striped wool appearing at intervals above and below the beadwork bands. Together, the beading and blanket stripes create an intricate geometric design motif. Beaded patterns in the form of letters, triangles, and horizontal and vertical bands are framed by heavy, black, beaded outlines. At bottom, the blanket is finished with a narrow length of fringe.

MARRIED WOMAN'S BLANKET CAPE (NGURARA)

Mid-20th century

Artist Unidentified
Ndebele region, South Africa
Middelburg wool blanket, glass beads, and string
Gift of Aaron and Joanie Young, Baltimore,
BMA 2002.631

Ndebele region, South Africa

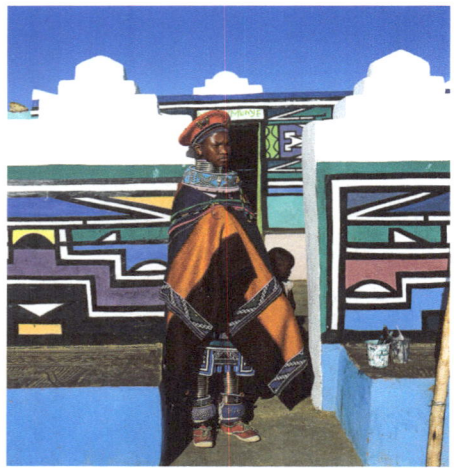

Sara Mthimunye wearing a front waist garment. Ndebele, South Africa.
Photo: © Margaret Courtney-Clarke, 1986

ART IN CONTEXT

THIS LESSON FEATURES WORKS OF ART made by Ndebele, Asafo, and Ejagham people living under Dutch or British colonial rule. The objects represent ways in which ethnic identity can be asserted through visual expression when one's culture is threatened. They may criticize or satirize changes in society as a result of colonial rule or reflect the melding of traditions that occurs as different cultures interact.

Over the centuries, the Ndebele were stripped of rights by white South African settlers. In the 1880s, following prolonged fighting, the land-holding Ndebele were defeated by the Boers (descendants of early Dutch settlers). Their ancestral lands were distributed to Boer farmers, and their people were indentured as laborers on Boer farms. Disruption and relocation continued, particularly between 1948 and 1994, when policies of segregation were enforced through apartheid. The goals of apartheid—meaning "separateness" in Afrikaans (pronounced AfriCAHNS), a language spoken by Boers and their descendants—were to segregate the nonwhite majority from the white minority and split black South Africans along ethnic lines to decrease their political power. More than 80 percent of the land was set aside for the white minority. The other 20 percent was divided into 10 "homelands," called "bantustans," (pronounced BANtustans) of Kwandebele (pronounced KWANdeBELay), where the Ndebele were relocated. Black South Africans were forcibly removed from their farms to these homelands, and the government sold the remaining land to white farmers. By the end of apartheid in 1994, when the system was abolished, more than 3.5 million people had been relocated.[1] Today, the majority of Ndebele live in the former bantustans of Kwandebele and Lebowa, located approximately 40 to 80 miles northeast of Pretoria, South Africa.[2]

Ndebele women responded to dislocation, marginalization, and loss of cultural traditions caused by Dutch colonial and apartheid regimes by asserting their identities through increasingly complex mural painting and beadwork.[3] As a visible affirmation of heritage and personal expression, women paint colorful murals of bright, abstract, predominantly flat designs, which are outlined in black with little overlap, directly on their homesteads. This distinctive patterning began around 1948 with the introduction of apartheid.[4] Originally these painted designs, perceived by the white majority to be purely decorative, were used by the Ndebele to communicate resistance through a complex visual language known only to them. Still painted today, these murals act as an affirmation of cultural identity.

The designs on an Ndebele blanket are borrowed from mural painting and vice versa. Worn as a cape by a bride or married woman (only on special occasions), a heavily decorated blanket weighs up to 10 pounds.[5] Testament to a woman's artistic abilities, a beaded blanket is a signifier of social status as well as a means of income. Once the Ndebele were forced off their land, women had few avenues for making money; beadwork became an important revenue generator. Both beadwork and mural painting are art forms practiced by married Ndebele women, and the patterns are taught by a mother to her daughter.

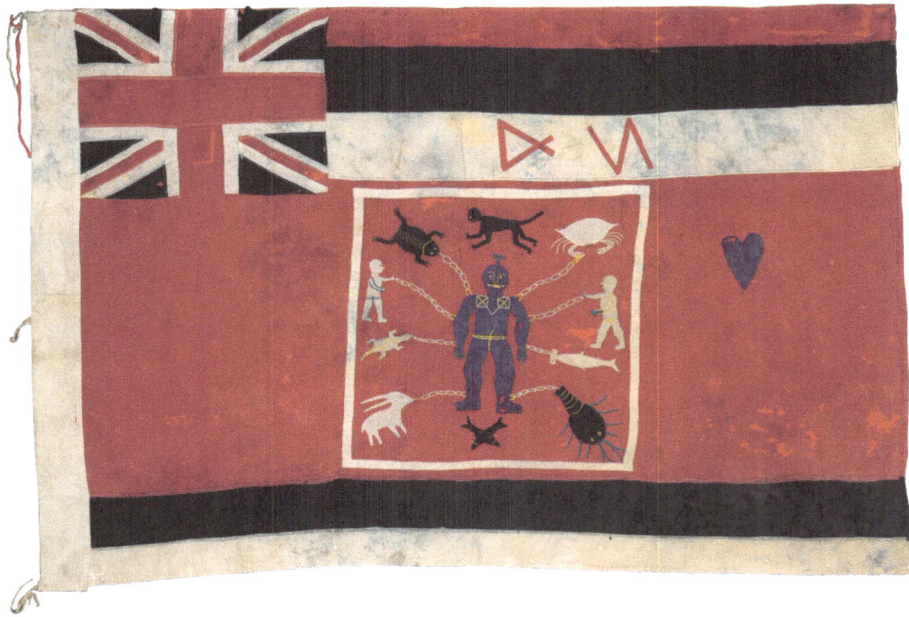

ASAFO MILITIA FLAG (FRANKAA)
Early to mid-20th century

Artist Unidentified
Fante region, Ghana
Cloth
Gift of Dawn M. Liberi, Washington, D.C.,
 BMA 1998.373

RELATED ARTWORK

SINCE THE 17TH CENTURY, appliquéd and embroidered flags called *frankaa* (pronounced FRENkah), have been commissioned by Fante men of coastal Ghana for militia companies. Historically, militias, called *Asafo*, served as a defense against threats from neighboring forces such as the Dutch-supported Ashanti, who controlled much of the territory of Ghana before the British arrived in the early 19th century. A close, though fraught, association between the Fante and the British colonials grew as their forces banded together to fight the Ashanti, who were often in conflict with them.

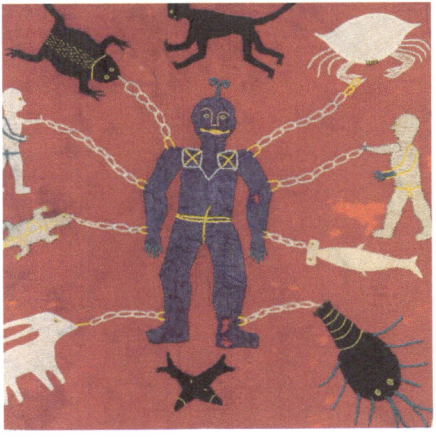

Detail of *Asafo* Militia Flag

By the late 19th century, the threat of invasion decreased, and the function of the Fante Asafo became more social than martial. Today, companies compete for bragging rights against neighboring units primarily through flag performances. Ceremonies occur at funerals of company members, festivals, or events honoring visiting dignitaries. The flag is carried by a militia member in performances that often recount past battles.[6]

> The dancer may unfurl the flag, flash it to the enemy, and then lie down and sleep on it to express confidence in eventual success…. Some steps are simply marvelous aesthetic embellishments—leaps, jumps, hops on one foot, twirls, and other flourishes—demonstrating the virtuosity of the dancer and heightening the entertainment value…. Upon the success of the "battle," the flag is paraded victoriously.[7]

Asafo flags are decorated with symbols that express particular militias' identities.[8] Some imagery was appropriated from the colonizing British Empire. On the BMA flag, a Union Jack, the national flag of the United Kingdom, is sewn in the upper left corner. It dates the frankaa to the early to mid-20th century, before Ghana gained independence in 1957. The meanings of the indigo heart, red linear designs on a white stripe, and enigmatic image of a man chained to animals and other figures remain cryptic. Generally, however, frankaa imagery is allegorical or historical in nature and can include boasts, insults, praise and inside jokes appreciated only by members of a specific Asafo.[9]

THE HELMET MASK has two faces, one red, representing a female, and one black, representing a male. The pairing of the two genders on one mask is a form developed by Ejagham artists of the Cross River delta region in southeast Nigeria. Both faces have front teeth carved to create triangular holes in the mouths through which maskers could see

Mounted on the helmet are four carved figures. Two are white British colonial males, identified by their uniforms, who face forward and backward above the red and black faces. A dark-skinned female figure, identified by her elaborate hairstyle as a local woman, faces to one side. Facing the other way is a dark-skinned male, presumably Ejagham, who wears a uniform and cap associated with the Nigerian police force. His position would have been appointed by the British government to enforce local colonial law.

The four carved figures represent people who would have been familiar in Ejagham society. The British Empire controlled the area from 1885 to Nigerian independence in 1960. British officers were a ubiquitous presence, as were the Ejagham police officers they hired. Given

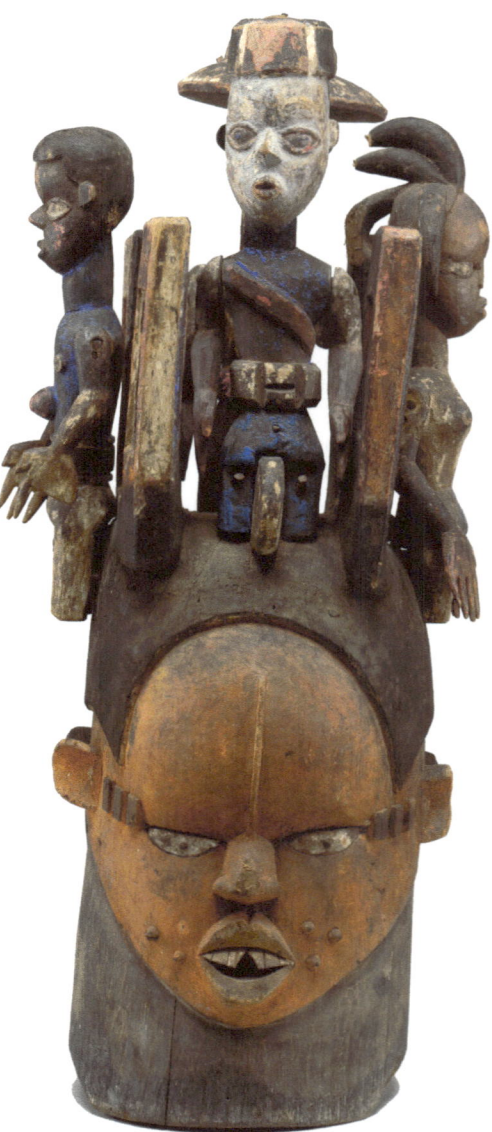

Artist Unidentified
Ejagham region, Nigeria
Wood, paint, pigment, and iron
Gift of Barry and Toby T. Hecht, Bethesda, Maryland, BMA 1990.161

the mix of the British figures, the Ejagham man in British uniform, and the Ejagham woman, the mask was probably worn in satirical performances that poked fun at cultural difference and criticized changes in society occurring under foreign rule.

[1] "Apartheid," History Network, accessed February 10, 2015, http://www.history.com/topics/apartheid/print.

[2] "Ndebele," Encyclopedia.com, accessed April 7, 2015, http://www.encyclopedia.com/topic/Ndebele.aspx.

[3] Sabine Marschall, "Sites of Identity and Resistance: Urban Community Murals and Rural Wall Decoration in South Africa," African Arts 35, 3 (Autumn 2002): 46.

[4] "The Influence of Apartheid," South African History Online, accessed February 13, 2015, http://www.sahistory.org.za/influence-apartheid.

[5] Frederick John Lamp, "The Body as Billboard: Ndebele Beadwork," in See the Music Hear the Dance, ed. Frederick John Lamp (Munich: Prestel Publishing, 2004), 48.

[6] Doran H. Ross, "We Will Fight You Day or Night: a Fante Flag (Frankaa)," in See the Music Hear the Dance, ed. Frederick John Lamp (Munich: Prestel Publishing, 2004), 82.

[7] Doran H. Ross, Fighting with Art: Appliquéd Flags of the Fante Asafo (Los Angeles: Fowler Museum of Cultural History, UCLA, 1979), 11.

[8] "New Materials and Contexts," University of Iowa Museum of Art, accessed February 3, 2015, http://africa.uima.uiowa.edu/chapters/cultural-exchange/new-materials-and-contexts/.

[9] "Regalia," University of Iowa Museum of Art, accessed February 2, 2015, http://africa.uima.uiowa.edu/chapters/governance/regalia/?start=5.

CLASSROOM ACTIVITIES

ACTIVITY 1:
Exploring Responses to Apartheid
Grades: 6–8
Subjects: English Language Arts, History/ Social Studies, Visual Arts

Within a unit that explores the South African policy of apartheid and its effects, students will examine the Married Woman's Blanket Cape and respond to the following questions. The teacher will record responses on the black/white board.

- At first glance, what do you notice most about the work?
- Describe the art elements—line, color, shape, texture, space, and form—that you see in this work.
- What patterns can you find in the work? Describe them.
- Do the patterns in this work look similar to anything you've seen before? If so, what does it remind you of and what makes it similar?

As students are sharing their responses, the teacher will offer relevant information about the object, being sure to include its origin and purpose, as well as the role of the patterns in communicating Ndebele identity in defiance of being marginalized and stripped of rights in South Africa.

Individual students will use print and/or online resources to select and research one other cultural group in South Africa that was affected by apartheid (such as the Zulu) and explore the different ways that the group asserted its identity and protested (such as songs, political protests, etc.). They will share their research in oral reports to the class using visual, video, and/or audio resources, and introduce a new question they have developed regarding their topic. The teacher will then lead the class in a discussion about the range of responses to apartheid.

ACTIVITY 2:
Examining Art and Identity
Grades: 6–8
Subjects: English Language Arts, History/ Social Studies, Visual Arts

The teacher will divide students into groups of four and provide each group with markers and a sheet of large paper. The teacher will ask the groups to brainstorm and respond to the following question, recording their answers on the paper.

- What are some ways that people express their identities visually— as individuals and as groups? (For example, wearing a team hat.)

The teacher will post the sheets from each group and ask students to share examples in discussion. The teacher will then share copies of the images of the Married Woman's Blanket Cape, the Asafo Militia Flag, and the Helmet Mask. Students will examine and discuss the objects, guided by questions:

- At first glance, what do you notice most about the works?
- Describe the art elements—line, color, shape, texture, space, and form—that you see in these works.
- Do any elements you see in the works look similar to anything you've seen before? If so, what are they and what makes them similar?

Students will then individually write up to five questions they have about the images, selecting one question to share with the class. The teacher will record it on the black/white board, offering relevant information in response. The teacher will include information about the objects' connections to group identities if the topic did not come up through the previous discussion.

Using posterboard, paper collage materials, glue sticks, and markers (if desired), student groups of four will collage class flags, using images and symbols to represent important aspects of the class. Groups will then present their flags, explaining the elements included in the image.

STANDARDS AND CURRICULUM

COMMON CORE STATE STANDARDS

English Language Arts
Grade 6
CCSS.ELA-Literacy.SL.6.1. Engage effectively in a range of collaborative discussions (one-on-one, in groups, and teacher-led) with diverse partners on grade 6 topics, texts, and issues, building on others' ideas and expressing their own clearly.

Grade 7
CCSS.ELA-Literacy.SL.7.1. Engage effectively in a range of collaborative discussions (one-on-one, in groups, and teacher-led) with diverse partners on grade 7 topics, texts, and issues, building on others' ideas and expressing their own clearly.

CCSS.ELA-Literacy.SL.7.4. Present claims and findings, emphasizing salient points in a focused, coherent manner with pertinent descriptions, facts, details, and examples; use appropriate eye contact, adequate volume, and clear pronunciation.

CCSS.ELA-Literacy.SL.7.5. Include multimedia components and visual displays in presentations to clarify claims and findings and emphasize salient points.

CCSS.ELA-Literacy.W.7.7. Conduct short research projects to answer a question, drawing on several sources and generating additional related, focused questions for further research and investigation.

Grade 8
CCSS.ELA-Literacy.SL.8.1. Engage effectively in a range of collaborative discussions (one-on-one, in groups, and teacher-led) with diverse partners on grade 8 topics, texts, and issues, building on others' ideas and expressing their own clearly.

MARYLAND STATE CURRICULUM

History/Social Studies
Grade 7
2.A.1.a. Apply understandings of the elements of culture to the studies of modern world regions, such as art, music, religion, government, social structure, education, values, beliefs, and customs.
2.B.1.a. Identify cultural groups within a contemporary world region.
2.C.1.a. Evaluate causes of conflict in the global community, such as Apartheid, the acquisition of natural resources, the decline of communism, ethnic persecution, and domestic and international terrorism.

Visual Arts
Grade 6
1.3.a. Identify and describe how artists use design concepts to organize the elements of art and principles of design to convey ideas, thoughts, and feelings.
2.1.a. Compare stylistic methods used by artists of different cultures to communicate feelings, ideas, and universal themes.
2.2.a. Identify historical, social, and cultural themes in selected artworks that influence the beliefs, customs, or values of a society.
2.2.b. Plan artworks based on historical, cultural, or social themes to communicate personal beliefs, customs, or societal values.

Grade 7
1.3.a. Compare and describe how artists use design concepts to organize the elements of art and principles of design to convey ideas, thoughts, and feelings in selected artworks.
2.1.a. Identify the roles and functions of the visual arts in expressing ideas, events, and universal themes within and among cultural groups.
2.2.a. Describe historical, social, and cultural themes in selected artworks that communicate beliefs, customs, or values of a society.
2.2.b. Plan artworks that use symbolic image and forms to convey selected beliefs, customs, or values.
2.3.a. Describe subject matter, styles, and techniques representative of various cultures and periods of art history.

Grade 8
1.3.a. Analyze why artists may select specific design concepts to convey meaning in artistic exemplars.
2.1.a. Analyze the roles and functions of the visual arts in expressing ideas, events, and universal themes within and among cultural groups.

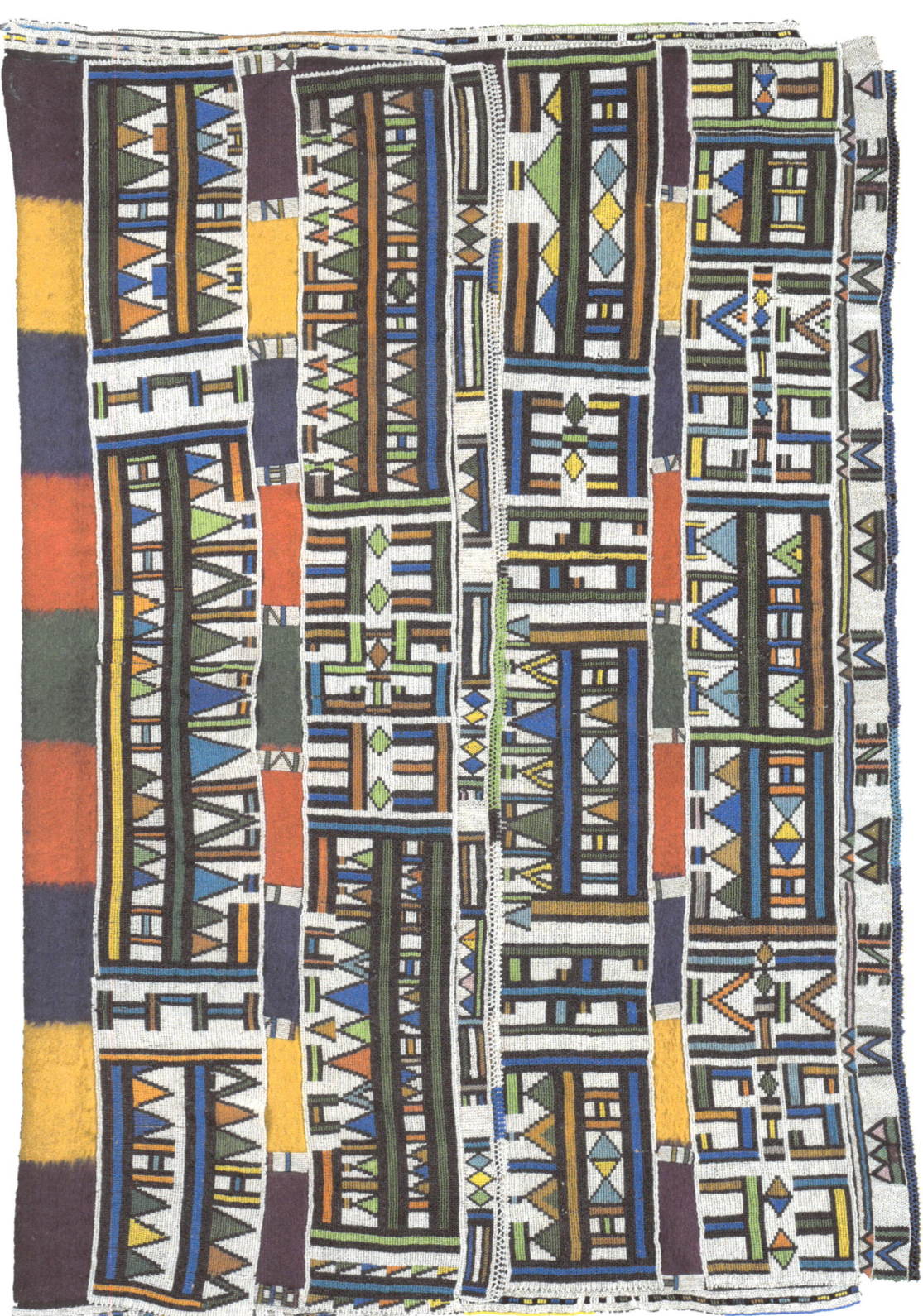

Married Woman's Blanket Cape (Ngurara). Mid-20th century, Ndebele region, South Africa. Middelburg wool blanket, glass beads, and string. Gift of Aaron and Joanie Young, Baltimore, BMA 2002.631

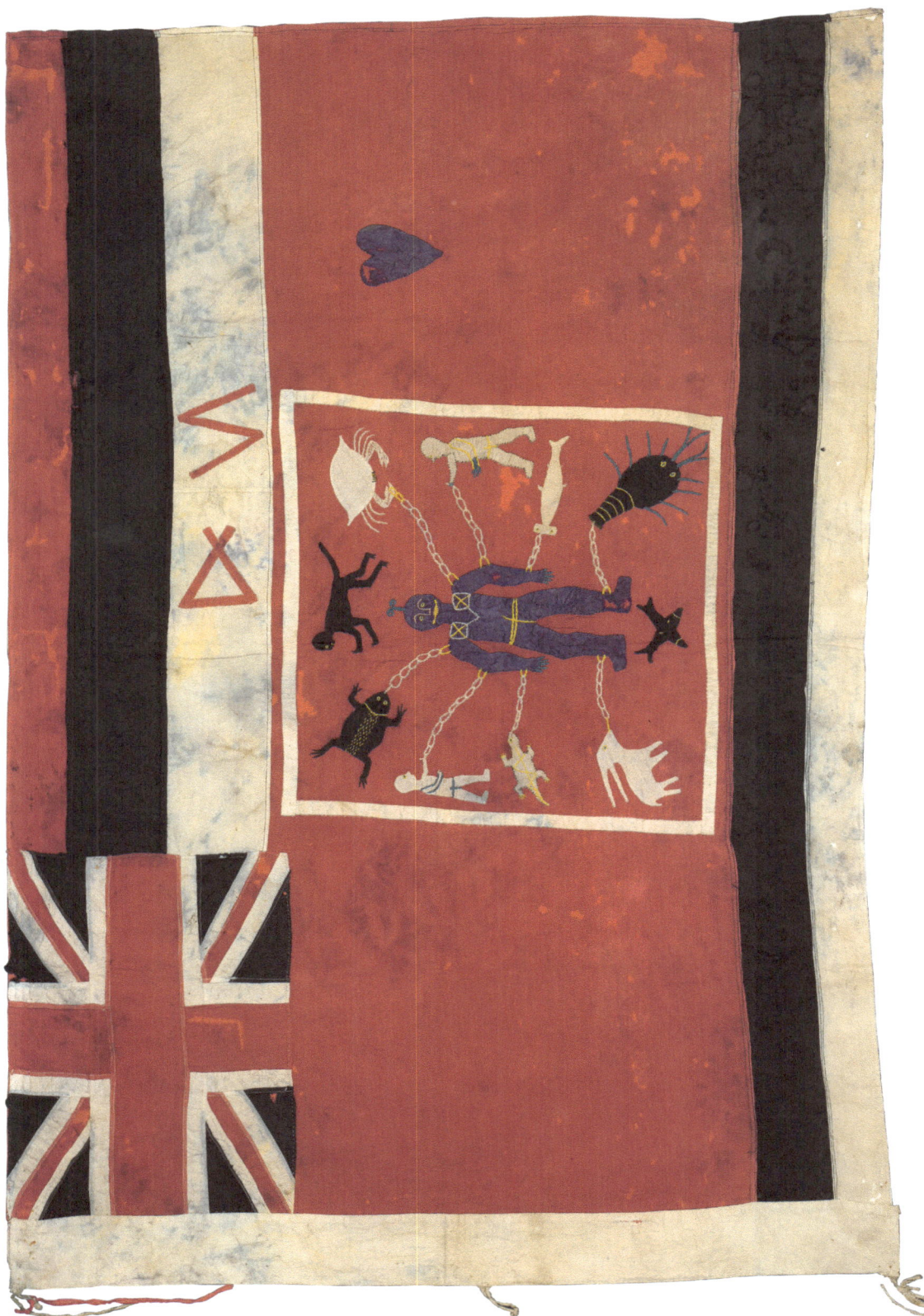

Asafo Militia Flag (Frankaa). Early–mid 20th century. Fante region, Ghana. Cloth. Gift of Dawn M. Liberi, Washington, D.C., BMA 1998.373

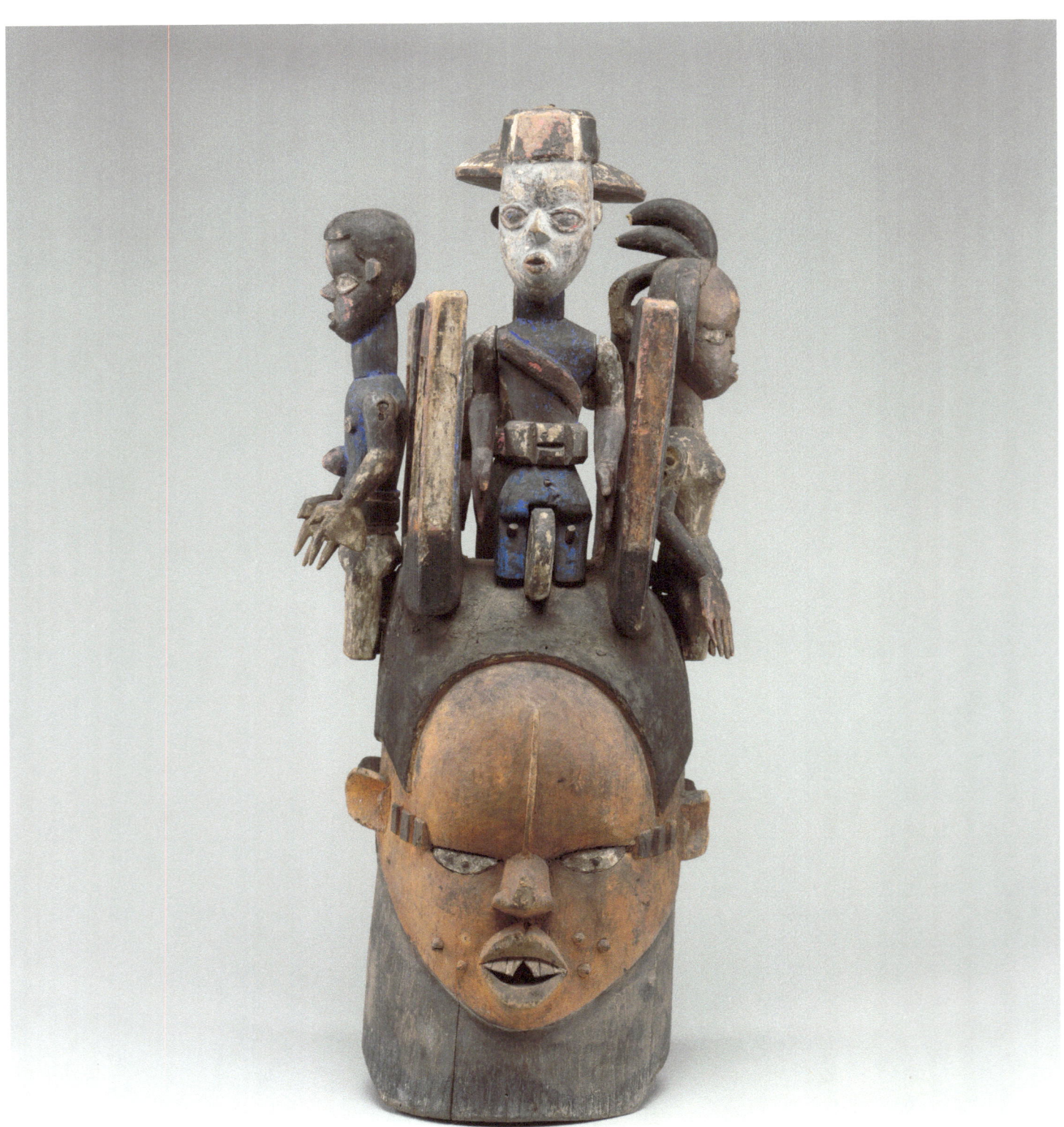

Helmet Mask. Mid-20th century. Ejagham region, Nigeria. Wood, paint, pigment, and iron. Gift of Barry and Toby T. Hecht, Bethesda, Maryland, BMA 1990.161

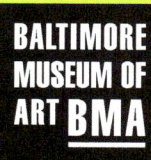

ART IN THE SPIRIT WORLD

BALTIMORE MUSEUM OF ART BMA

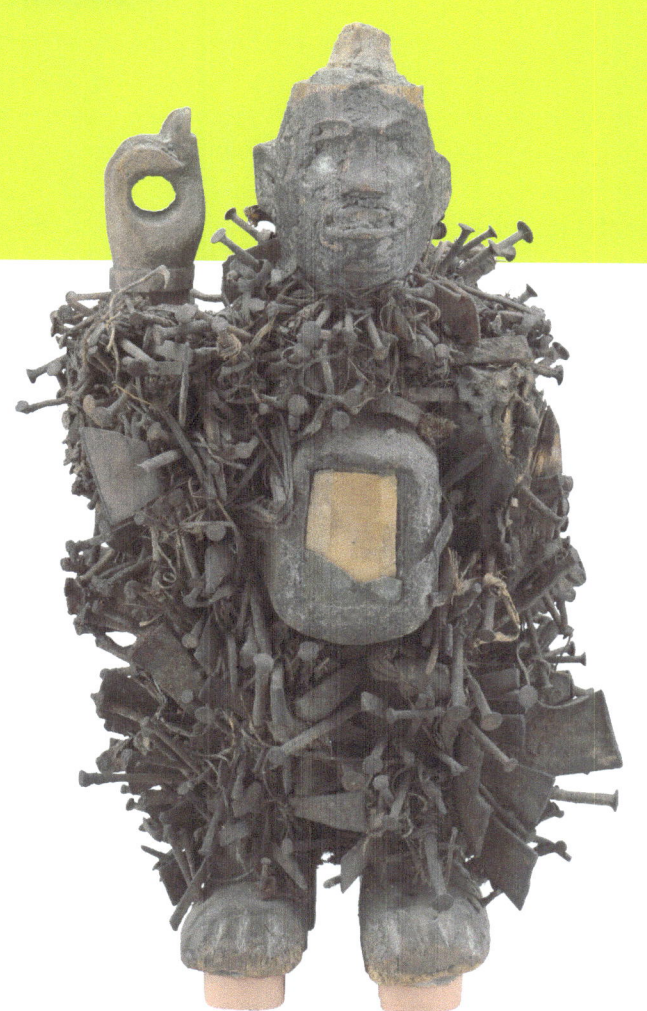

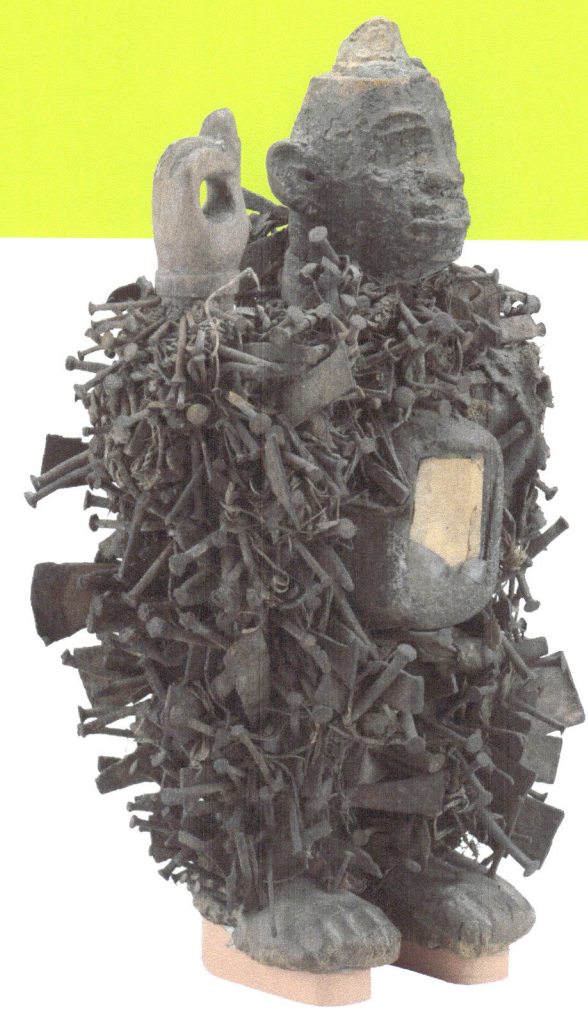

CLOSE LOOKING

CARVED OF WOOD FOR A KONGO (pronounced KONgo) ritual specialist, this Power Figure was made in the Democratic Republic of the Congo in the 18th century. The wide-eyed figure, called an Nkisi (pronounced enKIsee), once held a weapon in its raised right hand. Hammered iron blades, pins, and nails in various sizes are embedded in its surface. Bits of raffia and twine that were once part of longer pieces of fiber are visible among the nails. The Nkisi wears a crested hairstyle, resembling a rooster's comb. The eyes are made of glass, and the figure has a mirrored glass at its navel.

POWER FIGURE (NKISI)
19th century

Artist Unidentified
Kongo kingdom, Democratic Republic of the Congo or Angola
Wood, iron, mirrored glass, earth, encrustation, fiber, and cloth
Gift of Alan Wurtzburger,
BMA 1954.145.66

ART IN CONTEXT

THE THREE FIGURAL OBJECTS in this lesson express aspects of the spiritual beliefs of their communities. Though the objects themselves do not have power, they serve as vessels to which spirits are called in order to assist the earthly realm. They may also remind individuals of their connections to ancestors who reside in the spiritual domain. Diviners mediate between the physical and ancestral worlds in order to predict events and seek answers to village concerns. For these occasions, Kongo diviners use strong medicines of herbs and roots to call upon spirits to inhabit the Power Figure. During the ceremony, nails and blades are hammered into the figure to activate its authority and add to its imposing presence. Spirits, through the Nkisi, might witness legal contracts, resolve conflicts, combat evil, or fight illness. For oaths and contracts, the parties might hammer nails as well as wrap the Nkisi with pieces of raffia and string to bind the agreement. The power of the Nkisi can also be used for negative purposes, perhaps to exact revenge or kill a rival.[1] The large number of nails in the BMA Nkisi attests to its frequent use by the diviner and its power when activated by spirits. When the Power Figure was not in use, the diviner stored it secretly with a cache of medicines.

The mirrored glass on the figure's belly can be understood in several ways. A mirror evokes the still surface of water that Kongo identify as the division between this world and the domain of the ancestors.[2] The flash of the mirror in sunlight deflects negative energy and evil away from the ceremony and indicates the spiritual force that is called on during mediation. The figure's wide glass eyes reference the spirit living within. The significance of the hairstyle resembling a rooster's comb lies in the rooster's crowing to announce the day at first light. The evocation of the comb in the Power Figure symbolizes the diviner's ability to shed light on or interpret difficult matters.[3]

The Kongo people, united by a common language, live along a 300 mile stretch of the Atlantic Coast from Congo, through Democratic Republic of the Congo, and south to northern Angola. The Kongo kingdom was founded in the 14th century and ended when it was colonized by the Portuguese in 1885. Later, a Kongo political party played an important role in helping the Democratic Republic of the Congo achieve independence in 1960, though unrest continues. The Democratic Republic of the Congo is the second largest country in Africa behind Sudan and is rich in natural resources including diamonds, cobalt ore, and copper.

Kongo kingdom, Democratic Republic of the Congo or Angola

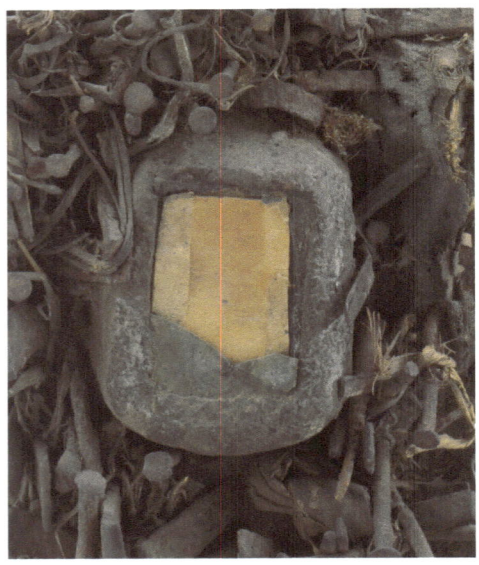

Detail of Power Figure (Nkisi)

RELATED ARTWORK

LARGE, CARVED MALE AND FEMALE SENUFO (pronounced senUfoh) figures from Côte d'Ivoire, called "Initiated Persons" or "They Who Gave Birth," represent ancestral couples. The figures appeared until the 1980s[4] at the initiation rites and deaths of male members of Pòrò, a primarily male governing body that allows young girls and post-menopausal women—two groups outside of childbearing years—to join.[5] During burial ceremonies that lasted four or five days, figures were carried through the village by masked dancers and placed at funeral sites. There, the couple was watched over by young initiates. The figures were considered witnesses to all events and represented living society members as well as Pòrò ancestors.   The ritual scarification marks, marking puberty, and full breasts of this Pòròpya (pronounced POROpeeha) speak of Senufo womanhood and motherhood. She stood as a metaphor for family both in this and the spiritual world and reminded villagers that the ancestors were never far away. A commanding presence, she, like all female ancestral figures, is taller than her male counterpart.[6]

When not in use, ancestral couples were stored standing up, as they were when on display in the village. Because of this, the lower parts of the figures were at risk of decay caused by insects and weathering, the result of which is evident in the BMA example.[7]

The name Côte d'Ivoire, meaning Ivory Coast, was coined by French merchants in the 16th century and reflected the nation's largest trading commodity—ivory. The area became a French protectorate in 1843, was formed into a French colony, and gained independence in 1960. Senufo are located in northern Côte d'Ivoire (and in Burkina Faso and Mali), and their towns are divided along matrilineal lines. Pòrò is one of four Senufo societies that helps regulate the actions of its citizens.

MANY BAULE (pronounced BOW—as in "take a bow"—lay) believe that when humans are born, they remain members of spirit families who reside in the ancestral world, called *blolo* (pronounced BLOHloh). During their lives, individuals are never entirely free from the spirits they leave behind. Sometimes spirit families look kindly on their human kin. However, sometimes *blolo* family members interfere negatively with life on earth. For example, a spirit wife may become jealous if her husband on earth marries. Her displeasure may be manifest in discord between the earthly spouses, infertility, or lack of prosperity.

In order to appease a spirit spouse, a Baule man or woman will have a flattering sculpture carved to represent his *blolo bla* (spirit wife) or *blolo bian* (spirit husband).[8] The figure is consecrated as a place for

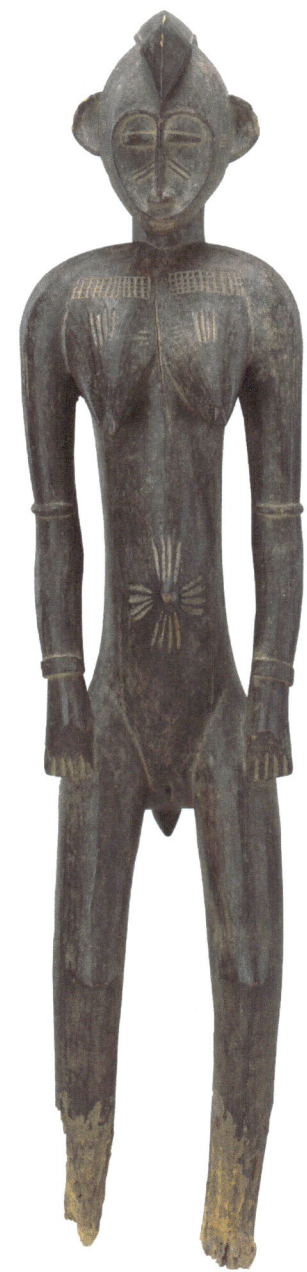

FEMALE ANCESTRAL FIGURE (PÒRÒPYA)
c. 1930

Artist Unidentified
Senufo region, Côte d'Ivoire
Wood
Purchase with Exchange Funds from Gift of Alan
Wurtzburger, BMA 1960.58

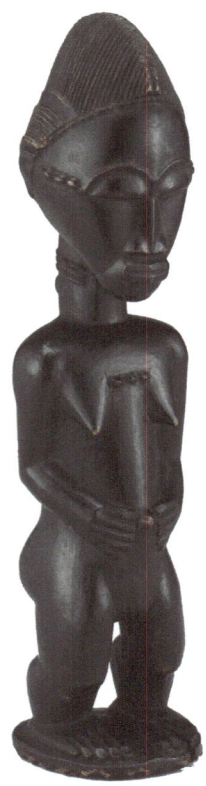

FEMALE SPIRIT SPOUSE (BLOLO BLA)
Early 20th century

Artist Unidentified
Baule region, Côte d'Ivoire
Wood
The Cone Collection, Formed by Dr. Claribel Cone and
Miss Etta Cone of Baltimore, Maryland, BMA 1950.384

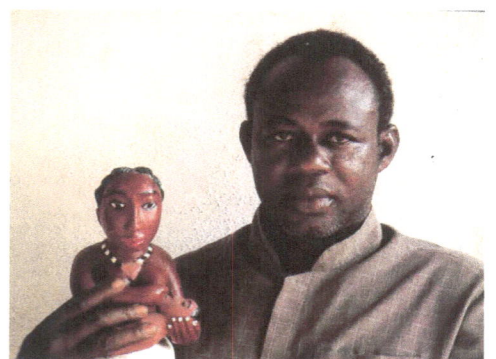

Kouassi Kouama and his spirit wife, Kami.
Photo: Susan M. Vogel, 1993

the spirit spouse to dwell and resides in a corner of the man or woman's sleeping room. As in the case of the BMA *blolo bla*, one night a week, the husband or wife would bring the carved figure to bed—in place of his or her spouse—to rest with overnight.

A Baule woman explains her relationship with her spirit husband:

> My blolo bian has his day when I sleep with him, and that day I do not sleep with my husband from here [on earth]…. [Before it was carved], we quarreled every day. We really quarreled! My spirit husband made me like that so I was always fighting with my husband. When I had it carved, calm returned to the house.
>
> A placated spirit can then spread good will to the earthly children and spouse of their partner and help confer health, money, and love. At the birth of a child or at another happy event, a man may give gifts of food or money to his wife's spirit husband to be used solely by the wife and spirit spouse. In this way, the ancestral world is never far from the earthly one.[9]

The Baule have a governing body run by a chief or king who inherits his position through the maternal line of the family and oversees subchiefs of local populations. Baule reside in central Côte d'Ivoire and are neighbors with the Senufo to the north.

[1] "Democratic Republic of the Congo; Kongo Peoples," University of Iowa Museum of Art, accessed March 11, 2015, http://uima.uiowa.edu/democratic-republic-of-the-congo-kongo-peoples-2/.

[2] Museum label for Power Figure (Nkisi), Baltimore, MD, The Baltimore Museum of Art, December 2009.

[3] Thompson, "Idiom of Clairvoyance, Healing, and Shared Moral Inquiry: a Kongo Figure (*Nkisi Lumweno*)," 258.

[4] During the 1960s and 1970s, thefts of Pòròpya increased so dramatically that replacing the figures became a financial burden for many societies. By the mid-1980s, figures had largely disappeared from funerals and were kept in society members' homes. Till Förster, "Weathering, Restoration, and Formal Criticism: a Senufo Figure (Pòròpya)," in *See the Music Hear the Dance*, ed. Frederick John Lamp (Munich: Prestel Publishing, 2004), 31.

[5] "Senufo," University of Iowa Museum of Art, accessed March 18, 2015, http://africa.uima.uiowa.edu/peoples/show/Senufo.

[6] Förster, "Weathering, Restoration, and Formal Criticism: a Senufo Figure (Pòròpya)," in *See the Music Hear the Dance*, ed. Frederick John Lamp (Munich: Prestel Publishing, 2004), 31.

[7] Ibid., 30.

[8] Susan Mullin Vogel, *Baule: African Art, Western Eyes* (New Haven, CT: Yale University Art Gallery, 1997), 67.

[9] Ibid., 248.

[10] Ibid., 258.

[11] "Baule," University of Iowa Museum of Art, accessed March 18, 2015, http://africa.uima.uiowa.edu/peoples/show/Baule.

CLASSROOM ACTIVITIES

ACTIVITY 1:
Exploring Power Figures
Grades: 9–12
Subjects: English Language Arts, Visual Arts

Students will examine the Power Figure (Nkisi), first making a basic sketch of the object. The teacher will then lead them in discussion using the following questions:

- At first glance, what do you notice most about the work?
- Describe the art elements—line, color, shape, texture, space, and form—that you see in this work.
- Are there elements in this work that you think you recognize? What are they?
- How is the human form presented in this work?

As students respond to questions, the teacher will provide relevant information about the object.

The teacher will then divide students into pairs and each pair will look at two additional Kongo Power Figures found on the following sites:

- http://www.metmuseum.org/toah/works-of-art/2008.30
- http://www.learner.org/courses/globalart/work/153/index.html

The pairs will then compare and contrast both figures with the BMA Power Figure (Nkisi) by sketching the figures individually, then engaging in a discussion. Students can use the following questions to help guide their exercise:

- Which art elements—line, color, shape, texture, space, and form— are similar in these works? Which are different?
- How is the human form presented in these two works? In what way are they similar? In what way are they different?
- What else is similar? Different?
- Can you find anything in the online information that accounts for any of the differences?
- What is the most interesting/intriguing thing you now know about Kongo Power Figures?

Teachers will then ask the student pairs to share their responses for a group discussion. The teacher will records the responses on the black/white board.

To extend this activity to an exploration of how one contemporary artist has referenced Power Figures, the teacher can present an image of the sculpture *Strange Fruit* by American artist Alison Saar, created in 2000, currently in the BMA contemporary collection. The teacher can project an image from BMA GoMobile and share information, such as the multimedia resources that support the exploration of the artwork (http://gomobileartbma.org/#object/7780), which include curatorial interviews and information on how Saar refers to a Power Figure's power pack in her sculpture.

- To which elements from a Power Figure did the artist (Alison Saar) refer in *Strange Fruit*?
- What is unique or different about the way she referenced these elements?
- How do the aesthetics connect these elements? How do the ideas connect these elements?
- Given what you understand now about Power Figures and *Strange Fruit*, what are some questions you have about either of the objects or their connections?

ACTIVITY 2:
Researching Religious Art
Grades: 9–12
Subjects: English Language Arts, Visual Arts

Students will look closely at the Power Figure (Nkisi), the Female Ancestral Figure (Pòròpya), and the Female Spirit Spouse (*blolo bla*). They will make basic sketches of each object and then following the sketching period, they will discuss their observations using the following questions as guidelines:

- At first glance, what do you notice most about the work?
- Describe the art elements—line, color, shape, texture, space, and form—that you see in this work.
- What are some elements in this work that you recognize?
- What are the different ways that the human form is represented in these works?

As students respond to the questions, the teacher will share relevant information about the objects provided in this guide. The teacher will then divide students into pairs and ask them to brainstorm other examples of figural religious artworks. Students will share their ideas in a larger class discussion. After the discussion, students will perform preliminary research to find figural religious works of art from any cultural tradition that they find compelling or interesting. (The teacher should ask students to be respectful in approaching works of art from living traditions. For some basic guidelines on how to talk about religious art, please visit: http://www.asia.si.edu/explore/ teacherResources/chola.connections.pdf, page 9.)

After doing in-depth research, each student will then write a three- to five-page essay about that artwork including its aesthetics, material and technical aspects, artist(s), audience(s), meaning(s), historical context, and any other relevant information, such as related works.

STANDARDS AND CURRICULUM

COMMON CORE STATE STANDARDS

English Language Arts
Grades 9–10
CCSS.ELA-Literacy.SL.9-10.1. Initiate and participate effectively in a range of collaborative discussions (one-on-one, in groups, and teacher-led) with diverse partners on grades 9-10 topics, texts, and issues, building on others' ideas and expressing their own clearly and persuasively.

CCSS.ELA-Literacy.SL.9-10.4. Present information, findings, and supporting evidence clearly, concisely, and logically, such that listeners can follow the line of reasoning and the organization, development, substance, and style are appropriate to purpose, audience, and task.

CCSS.ELA-Literacy.W.9-10.2. Write informative/explanatory texts to examine and convey complex ideas, concepts, and information clearly and accurately through the effective selection, organization, and analysis of content.

Grades 11–12
CCSS.ELA-Literacy.SL.11-12.1. Initiate and participate effectively in a range of collaborative discussions (one-on-one, in groups, and teacher-led) with diverse partners on grades 11-12 topics, texts, and issues, building on others' ideas and expressing their own clearly and persuasively.

CCSS.ELA-Literacy.SL.11-12.4. Present information, findings, and supporting evidence, conveying a clear and distinct perspective, such that listeners can follow the line of reasoning, alternative or opposing perspectives are addressed, and the organization, development, substance, and style are appropriate to purpose, audience, and a range of formal and informal tasks.

CCSS.ELA-Literacy.SL.11-12.7. Conduct short as well as more sustained research projects to answer a question (including a self-generated question) or solve a problem; narrow or broaden the inquiry when appropriate; synthesize multiple sources on the subject, demonstrating understanding of the subject under investigation.

MARYLAND STATE CURRICULUM

Essential Learner Outcomes
Visual Arts
Grades 9–12
Outcome II: Expectation A: Student will propose ways that visual art reflects significant historical, cultural, and social issues.

Outcome II: Expectation B: The student will determine factors that influence the creation of art in specific historical eras and places by studying artworks and other sources of information.

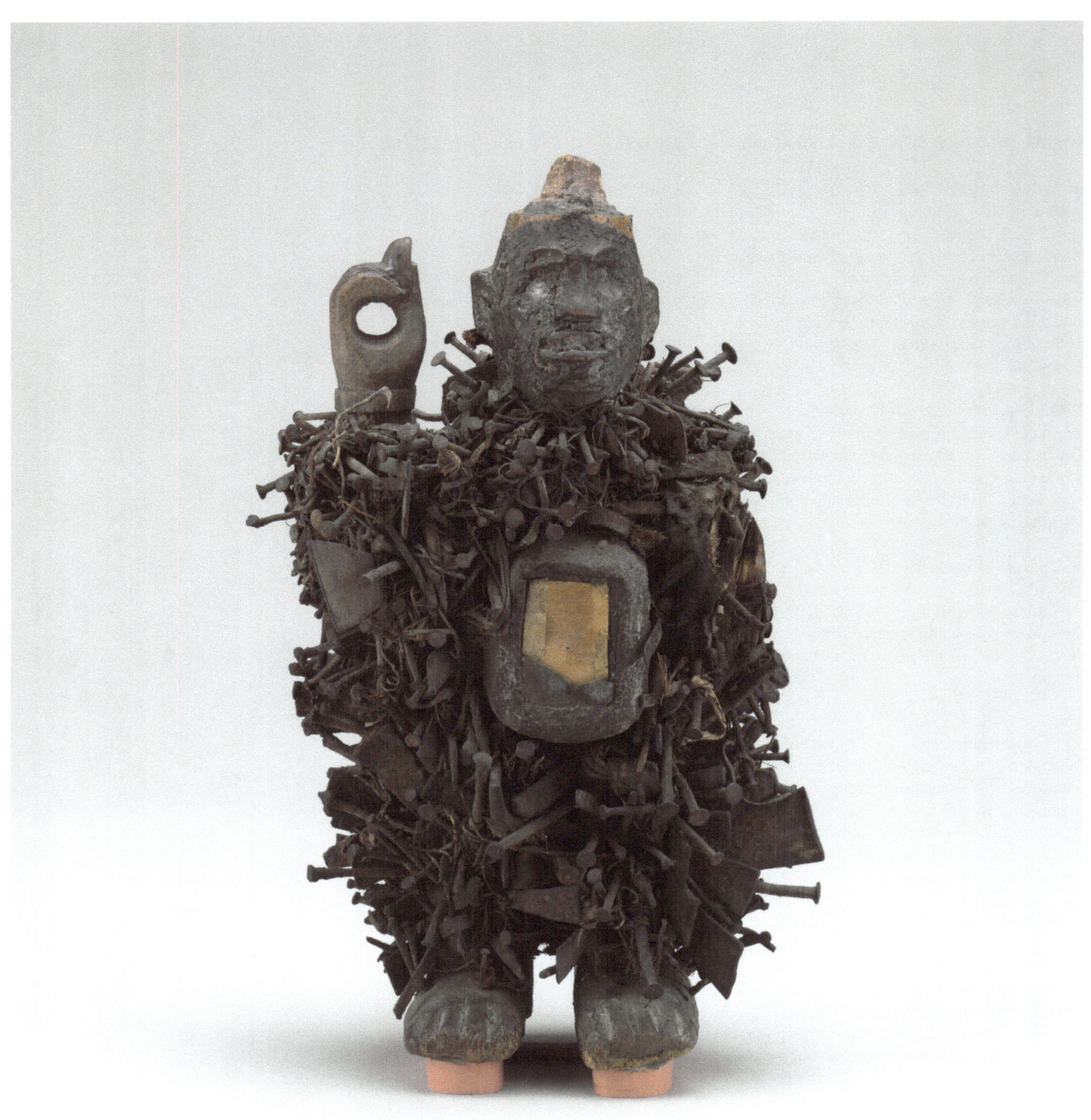

Power Figure (Nkisi). 19th century. Kongo kingdom, Democratic Republic of the Congo or Angola. Wood, iron, mirrored glass, earth, encrustation, fiber, and cloth. Gift of Alan Wurtzburger, BMA 1954.145.66

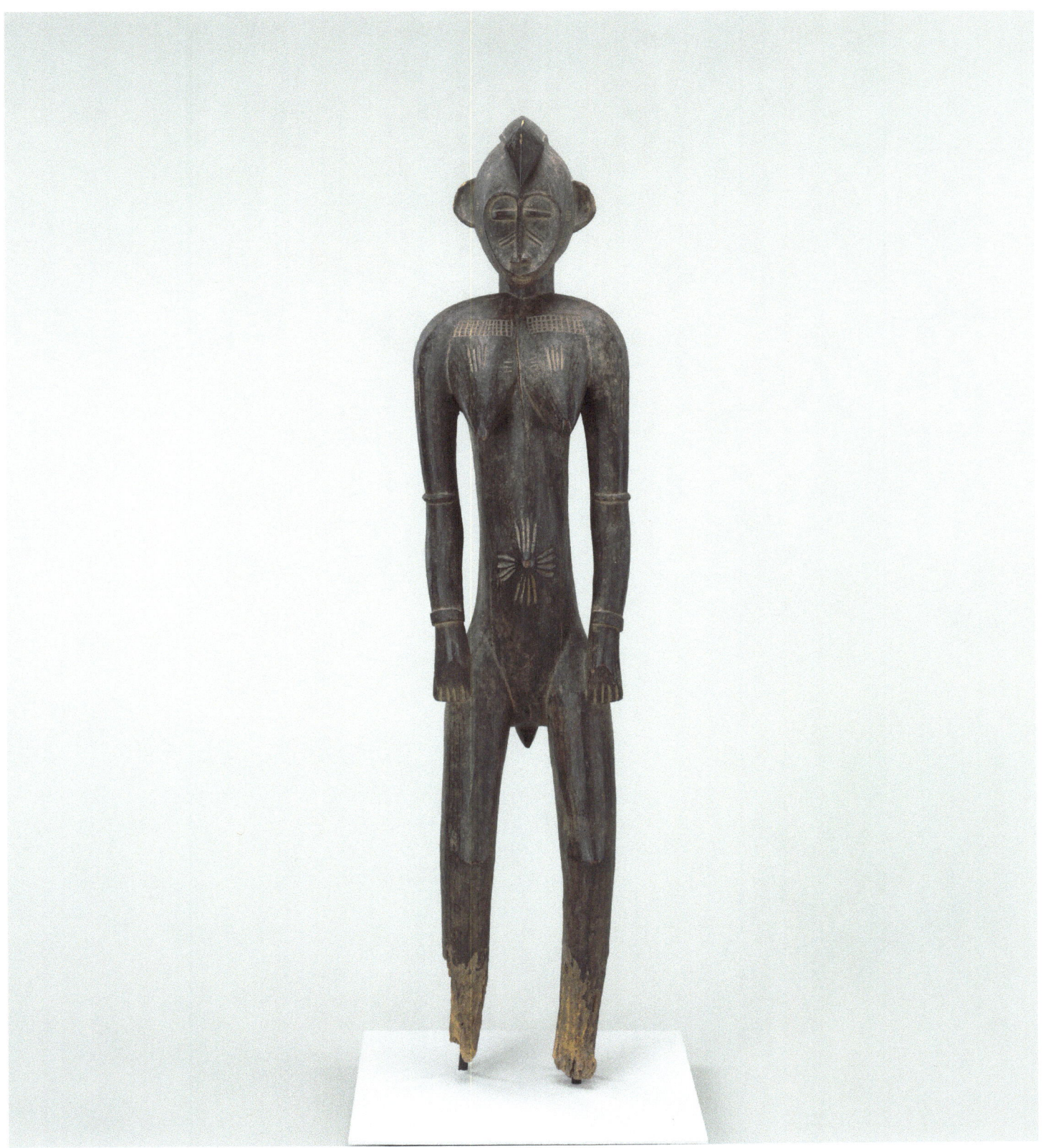

Female Ancestral Figure (Pòròpya). c. 1930. Senufo region, Côte d'Ivoire. Wood.
Purchase with exchange funds from Gift of Alan Wurtzburger, BMA 1960.58

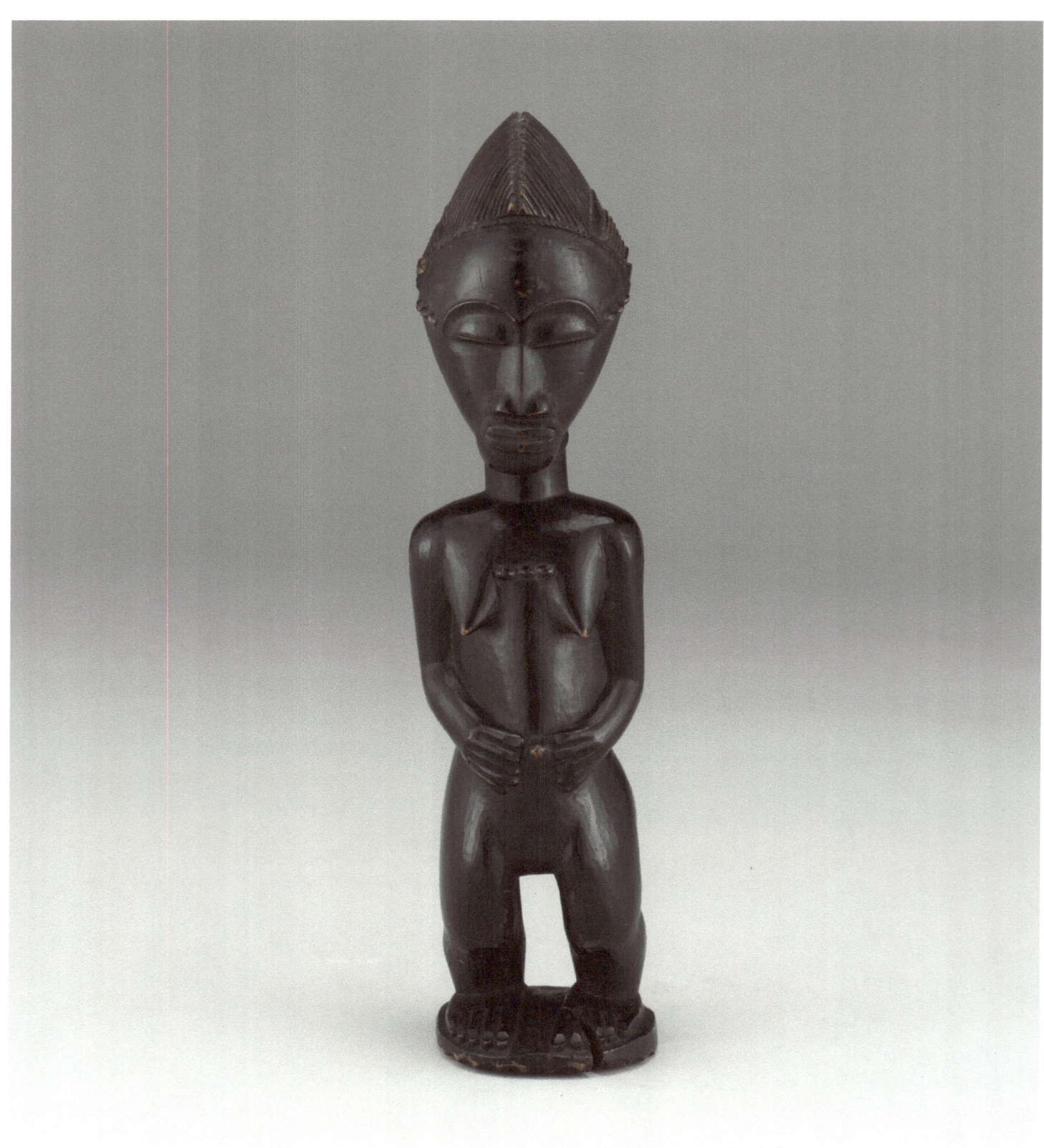

Female Spirit Spouse (Blolo Bla). Early 20th century. Artist Unidentified. Baule region, Côte d'Ivoire. Wood. The Cone Collection, Formed by Dr. Claribel Cone and Miss Etta Cone of Baltimore, Maryland, BMA 1950.384

www.ingramcontent.com/pod-product-compliance
Lightning Source LLC
Chambersburg PA
CBHW050857180526
45159CB00007B/2710